"From emotional mountaintops to the deepest valleys, Lee Blum takes you through the stark reality of life with an eating disorder. Her riveting account of real-life experiences and the hope found in her faith in God will leave you hanging on to every page. In my twenty years of experience treating eating disorders I have seen no other writing that offers more for the individual who desperately needs recovery."

Joel Jahraus, MD, FAED (Fellow of the Academy of Eating Disorders), eating disorder professional

"In a world where we are encouraged to hide our pain and ignore the brokenness around us, Lee Blum's *Table in the Darkness* is a tender, stark and vital reminder that so many in our midst struggle, and struggle deeply. Her story is horrific and hopeful, and the ultimate power of authentic community offers hope to all of us, regardless of what we carry around inside of us. With so few voices reminding us how deeply we need and long for one another, Lee Blum's is a godsend."

Chap Clark, Fuller Theological Seminary

"I am a huge fan of Lee Wolfe Blum. She is an inspiring example of the freedom that comes when we allow God's loving truth to seep through the cracks in our armor and nourish the deepest corners of our hearts. In *Table in the Darkness*, Lee reminds us that God is at work in us always, even—and often—when we're not looking."

Constance Rhodes, founder and CEO, FINDINGbalance; author, *Life Inside the "Thin" Cage*

"*Table in the Darkness* is a page-turning account of a woman's battle against mental illness and the inspiring story of how she overcomes. I couldn't put it down and cannot recommend it highly enough to those longing for freedom from their past."

Emily Wierenga, author of *Chasing Silhouettes*

"In *Table in the Darkness,* Lee Blum shows . . . that recovery and healing from the devastating effects of an eating disorder are possible. This book is a source of hope and instruction for those battling an eating disorder as well as for loved ones."

Kim Bushman, licensed psychologist, Water's Edge Counseling & Healing Center

"Having waged my own war with eating disorders, I identified with Lee's account of almost overwhelming struggles, and then the welcome outcome of a hard-won recovery. Her story is raw, real and revealing . . . a clear and victorious validation of the fact that recovery is possible."

Cherry Boone O'Neill, author of *Starving for Attention*

LEE WOLFE BLUM

table in the darkness

a healing journey through

an eating disorder

IVP Books

An imprint of InterVarsity Press
Downers Grove, Illinois

InterVarsity Press
P.O. Box 1400, Downers Grove, IL 60515-1426
World Wide Web: www.ivpress.com
Email: email@ivpress.com

InterVarsity Press® is the book-publishing division of InterVarsity Christian Fellowship/USA®, a
movement of students and faculty active on campus at hundreds of universities, colleges and schools of
nursing in the United States of America, and a member movement of the International Fellowship of
Evangelical Students. For information about local and regional activities, write Public Relations Dept.,
InterVarsity Christian Fellowship/USA, 6400 Schroeder Rd., P.O. Box 7895, Madison, WI 53707-7895,
or visit the IVCF website at www.intervarsity.org.

While all stories in this book are true, some names and identifying information in this book have been
changed to protect the privacy of the individuals involved.

Back cover photo of the author courtesy of heatherfenskephotography.com

Cover design: Cindy Kiple
Interior design: Beth Hagenberg
Image: woman with bandage over mouth: Fuse/Getty Images

ISBN 978-0-8308-4308-4 (print)
ISBN 978-0-8308-7186-5 (digital)

Printed in the United States of America ∞

Library of Congress Cataloging-in-Publication Data
A catalog record for this book is available from the Library of Congress.

P	18	17	16	15	14	13	12	11	10	9	8	7	6	5	4	3	2	1
Y	28	27	26	25	24	23	22	21	20	19	18	17	16	15	14	13

To my beloved husband and amazing boys,

I love you to the moon and back.

■ ■ ■

To the reader:

"My hope is that the description of

God's love in my life will give you the

freedom and the courage to discover

. . . God's love in yours."

HENRI NOUWEN
Here and Now: Living in the Spirit

contents

PROLOGUE

accident

"What did you take? Do you know how much? What did you take?"

The booming drum of his voice beat strong against my ears, "What did you take? What did you take?"

My throat, a box locked by a sharp pain, unable to be opened. Another voice, a different voice, was above me and asking the same question, barking at me: "You need to tell us what you took. We want to help you."

I remember: I don't want to be helped.

I want to return to the space of darkness—back in the ocean of it—floating freely into nothing. The pain begins to slip away, and I reach back to the edges of its humid air. I feel it washing over me and the words falling away in the distance.

"Lee?" They shake me. "Lee. What kind of pills did you take?"

Stop. Stop grabbing my arm, I scream inside. *Stop talking and let me be.*

But I am jolted from my nirvana of dark nothingness. A voice sounds familiar. Whose voice? Heavy with fear. Chris. Chris's voice.

My eyes open. I focus up on Chris towering above me. *Why is he here? Where is here?* Inside my heart punches at my chest when I see tears rolling down his face. *Why is he crying?*

"I want to sleep," I try to scream, but the sound refuses to come out of my mouth. So I constrict every part of me and push the sound out my prisoned throat: "LEAVE ME ALONE!"

The words are a garbled slur of incomprehensible speech, unheard.

I close my eyes in defeat and swim back in. Behind my eyes, I pass the dark into another layer with soft, blue ocean. I am free.

I hear my voice, quiet this time, a relaxed whisper pleading, "Please let me be."

life is like
an onion

I sat onstage faced by a red sea of hats atop the heads of the hundreds of high school graduates. Families and friends watched in the stands, escorting us through our rite of passage.

My report card was filled with success. And I was counting.

Papers shaking in my trembling hands, holding the speech I poured over and over until perfect. I closed my eyes and sipped in a breath of the muggy Kansas heat. I lightly brushed my blond hair, finally long, behind my shoulders as I listened—excited and nervous—to the other speeches. Being chosen to speak was an exclamation mark at the end of my constant striving to prove something. To prove I was not chained down by my family's expectation of who I was or should be. To prove that, while they were busy moving me to new houses and new schools, I was overcoming. I was proving that the voices telling me I wasn't good enough, that I didn't measure up, didn't affect me.

· I didn't know those voices would follow me.

The story I told myself was simple: college and then Broadway lights flashing my name. Dad was skeptical, constantly asking,

"How on earth do you expect to make money in theater?" I ignored his hesitation.

The petite principal peered over the lectern, her voice echoing in the speakers, "The oration this evening will be given by Ms. Lee Wolfe." I lift my eyes and spot my family sitting poised on the metal bleachers. They are proud of me. I see it in their smiles held wide. They smile and they look good, because looking good is important.

I see Mom with her blue eyes and soft smile. Mom knew how to sew patches where I made holes.

■　　■　　■

The split-level, butter-yellow house on 100th street in Kansas was my favorite home, the one I lived in the longest. A cozy, paneled room was where we lived, but we didn't call it a living room. It was a TV room, though it should have been called a waiting room. I did most of my waiting there, listening for The Voice while pretty ladies and men talked and kissed onscreen.

Lots of kissing.

Half-day kindergarten allowed me precious time alone with Mom on the long, brown couch while my older brother and sister stayed at school. But the kissing on the TV pulled her away from me. I was wiggly, always wiggly. I would move around the couch, trying to sit still: legs underneath like Mom, legs crossed, legs dangling over the big couch. I waited for The Voice to tell me about the sands and the hourglass: my cue that it was okay to talk, my cue to have Mom back from TV-land.

A large photo of me hung on the wall. I hated it. Mom and Dad said it was cute. The photo of me shows my bright blonde hair sticking out like a baby chick, my mouth wide open screaming, and then there were those cheeks—fat cheeks that carried my face. My brother's photo, on the other hand, was adorable—an image of him in a tuxedo when he was a ring bearer in a wedding.

My sister Kristin's photo hung on the other wall: an angelic image with her soft, blondish hair spread beautifully on her shoulders and a sweet smile on her face. Her hair could swoop over her shoulders just like Jan Brady. I wanted long hair like hers, but Mom always insisted I keep mine short.

She sat next to me, her shoulders back, her head up, her hair feathered perfectly on the sides in blond wisps that mingled gently with her golden curls. She is beautiful. Everyone says so. I always thought she was the prettiest Mom I had ever seen, except in the morning when she first woke up and smelled like stinky breath. Now her long, thin legs were tucked, and she held her sewing—my jeans with the knees ripped out again—in her lap. She sewed patches where I created holes.

Up and down, in and out, her eyes on the TV, Mom pulled the silver needle through the rough material. *How does she sew and watch TV?* I wondered. She wore her I-don't-want-to-be-bothered look: squeezing her soft, mauve lips like a wrinkled prune on one side of her face and stretching the other side of her cheek, while hard thoughts pinched her eyebrows together. I stayed and waited, holding my lips closed so I didn't catch a fly.

"Close your mouth or you are going to catch a fly!" she would scold.

I was a balloon ready to burst. The air was my words waiting to get out. I wanted Mom to help me now; I couldn't do this without her help.

I wanted to tie my shoes. Everyone else knew how. Why couldn't I? I tried, but my fingers got in the way. The loop would fall out of my hand and I would try and try again. I gave up, set

the shoe next to me and waited. I knew better than to talk before
The Voice said his line.

The air inside of me twirled and spun, and I wiggled my toes
and waited: big toe over the second toe, second toe over the big
toe, wiggle, wiggle, wiggle.

Somehow, at age five, I was always less than—in my own
mind—somehow failing. I didn't want to ask for help anymore.
I knew asking for help made me weak. And I hated it.

I waited for the hourglass, my tummy tight and in knots from
waiting. Finally, small sand appeared on the large screen,
pouring out of the hourglass. In his deep theater voice, the man
slowly said, "Like sands through the hourglass, so are the days
of our lives." I scooted close to Mom.

"Mom, Mom, Mom," I said quickly, holding my white tennis
shoes, gripping the rubber edges tight. Finally unlocked from
the mesmerizing gaze of the TV, her lips relaxed into a tender
smile. She was with me. Present. She looked down at me sitting
next to her, just now "seeing me."

"Yes, what is it?" she asked calmly.

"Mom. Mom. Please teach me how to tie my shoes. Please, I
hate having everyone do it for me. Please, Mom!" I whined.

She smiled softly at me, "Yes, honey." She offered her soft
hand out for my shoe. I scooched near her, my tummy loos-
ening: just the two of us, close and cozy. She smelled like
flowers. I hoped the man on the TV wouldn't interrupt again.
She pulled the long, white shoelaces up from my shoe and held
them out, showing me how to make a bow and where to put my
fingers. I watched. With my eyes wide open, my body leaning
into hers, listening, I took it all in. I practiced and Mom guided
me as I went, "Make the loop, now the other loop," she said
gently. "There you did it! See Lee, you can do it."

Her words of encouragement fueled the fire in me to do it right, to do it over and over again. And I did, and she watched, sometimes even putting her fingers on top of mine to help me along. I smiled up at her, proud of myself. In her shiny eyes I saw her proud of me too. She wrapped her right arm around me and squeezed me tight. On my head she planted a soft, tender kiss.

And then, out of the corner of my eye, the hourglass appeared again. Back to the TV. She collected her sewing, jerking the silver needle up and out, her eyes right back on that screen. I wondered where she disappeared to when she watched those people kissing and hugging. Why couldn't she be here? In our house? With me?

■   ■   ■

The principal continued, "Lee was president of the student congress this year and served as secretary of the student council last year. She was vice president of the thespian executive board and has performed in fourteen drama productions, winning the lead role in many of them. She also participated in the varsity drill team. Lee will attend Southwest Missouri State University in Springfield, Missouri. And she invites her classmates to fly. . . ."

Waiting for my turn to speak, I stood onstage with wobbly knees, and I suddenly felt faint. I had been known to faint. In grade school I got overheated while wearing a puffy, white snowsuit that zipped from my toes to my lips. I looked like the Michelin Man, but Mom told me to keep it on no matter what. I obeyed. But it was warm on the playground, and a layer of sweat began to grow between me and the suit. When the teacher blew her whistle and instructed us to line up, my vision blurred and my body fell back on the asphalt. Luckily for me, the snowsuit was so puffy it cushioned my fall, and I only suffered a light bump on my head. After school I told Mom about my embarrassing playground incident. She responded quickly, discounting the experience, "O Lee, stop exaggerating!"

So as I stood, gathering myself together, I tried to ignore the feeling that I might faint. I pictured myself like a freight train ready to barrel through anything that got in my way. *God loves me. I know he loves me*, I reminded myself. *If God loves me and he knows the plans he has for me—he declared it, after all—then wouldn't he want good things for me? I thought. Things like Broadway, cute boyfriends, lots of success and happiness? Right? Wouldn't he want that for me?*

■   ■   ■

My relationship with God had only begun the summer before at a Young Life camp, which I had gone to mainly to chase after a boy. Mom had told me to be careful before I left: not for snakes or broken bones, but for the brainwashing.

I wasn't worried about the brainwashing. I had started learning about *this* Jesus, and I had my own fears. I had seen those girls, the ones who loved Jesus. They wore their shirts buttoned up to their eyeballs, and they always seemed to wear headbands. Plus, they spent Friday nights reading the Bible.

"Do I have to give up beer?" I asked our chemistry teacher, Hutch, who went on the trip with us. We were sprawled out in the lobby of one of the cabins, playing cards. "And what about cussing? Do I have to give that up too?"

I remember him telling me that a relationship with God was about so much more than drinking beer. It was about loving God. I wasn't sure I believed him. But I was hungry, hungry for what the boy I was chasing had, hungry for what the leaders had. Was it a sureness about themselves or a peace? Or maybe it was their talk of something bigger, and someone who loved me for me. I told our teacher I was willing to think about the things he said at camp. But I wasn't going to stop drinking or saying bad words.

"Lee, God loves you for who you are, for the person he created you to be. He doesn't get all caught up in the things you get caught up in."

"We will see," I said. I didn't want rules. But a God who loved me for me, who wanted to talk with me, that I wanted.

A year later, on a dark night at camp, lit only by stars, I stood on a brown, curved footbridge, my elbows resting on the wood and my eyes fixed up at the sky. The world was so much bigger and so much more interesting with the idea of God, a God who looked at me, who cared about me. I felt weightless and unbound by my former fears of God. I took a long, deep breath of the cool air and said the words I had been hesitant to say: "God, I have made mistakes, and God, I gossip a lot. I even have really yucky thoughts about people sometimes. Will you forgive me? Will you come into my heart like the speaker said? Will you be my savior, whatever that means, God? I need you."

I wouldn't say the word *Jesus* yet, because it still reminded me of headbands and buttoned-up shirts, but I did know and understand then that there was something beyond me—and Someone I could trust to not leave me or hurt me.

■　■　■

I swallowed my nerves down and confidently approached the podium. After adjusting the microphone, I quoted Carl Sandburg: "Life is like an onion; you peel off one layer at a time." I delivered the speech looking into the faces of my classmates: "We have become young adults ready to step out into the future. And the future holds so much for each and every one of us. The choices available to us are innumerable. We live in a time where we can be or do anything that we want, and it is up to us to make these choices."

I said these words, not for them but for me. I had choices now, and launching off to college would open up opportunities and freedom unlike anything I had ever had. And it couldn't come fast enough: my opportunity to be whomever I wanted, to do whatever I wanted, to live the life I wanted to live. It would be wonderful, and exciting. I just knew it. I paused before my last line, "Life is like an onion; you peel off one layer at a time . . . and sometimes you weep."

on my own

Dad brought me on a hot, humid day in August, helping me lug my overstuffed suitcases up the dormitory stairs. We found our way to my room, the door decorated with a crafty welcome sign in swirly, cursive letters. "Here we are!" Dad said with relief. His face, a heated red, made his blue eyes shine even brighter. He opened the door to my room, placing the suitcases on the brown, tiled floor. I stood, looking into the tiny room, and thought of Alice in Wonderland, feeling much larger than the space in front of me. I imagined if I were to cry in this shrunken room, Dad and I might both have drowned.

I took a long breath and walked into the gap between the two beds, a path that only fit Dad, my suitcases and me. An open window carried in a sticky breeze and a wet moldy basement smell. I teetered between wanting Dad to leave so I could begin my new life and yearning for him to stay forever—to keep me safe, to protect me.

"Well, my youngest is leaving the nest," he joked, "My baby, finally on her own." I was waiting for the other lines he had said so often, "the *other* child" or "the accident," but he didn't say them. He just continued, now serious, "My baby girl is all grown up!"

"Aww, Dad," I responded, my cheeks hot, remembering days of Saturday soccer games and donuts in the park.

■   ■   ■

There were church Sundays and then there were donut Sundays. Church Sundays happened mostly during holidays or when we had newly ironed outfits to show off. Dad was never one to sleep in, so I always knew I could find him early—with coffee and a morning paper at our kitchen table. When I woke, I would quickly change out of my Garfield nightgown, slip into my Jordache jeans and a T-shirt, and tiptoe downstairs. Dad would be there at the round table, the place where he had often said, "Tables aren't made for five. Roller coasters aren't made for five."

I knew the five. I was the five, the "accident" in a family of four, ripping its tidy seams open. That didn't matter on those mornings, and I brushed those thoughts away. What mattered was Dad and donuts.

If I was up before the others I would practically jump into dad's lap with excitement. He would swallow me up in his embrace, his strong arms wrapped around me. In his red or blue collared shirt, with his hair combed like he just came from the barber, his blue eyes would catch mine and he would whisper, "Should we get some donuts today?"

"Yes!" I would squeal, jumping up and down while still trying to be quiet enough so it would just be Dad and me.

But, some mornings he would be a crabapple and wouldn't talk much, just reading the paper and drinking coffee. Those were nondonut days. On donut days, though, Dad would stand up, pushing the chair behind him while I burst into the hall to grab my tennies.

A chime sounded when we entered the Dunkin' Donuts store,

full of sugary sweet smells. It was empty except for those working there, and I knew we had beaten the church crowd. "Early bird catching the worm," Dad would say, winking. I walked up to the big, rounded case, placed my hands on the warm glass and peered into it, searching for my favorite donut: a cream-filled chocolate éclair. I pointed to it and looked at Dad for his nod of approval.

With my éclair, glazed donuts for him and chocolate milks for both of us, we were off. We drove to a huge park with miles of windy roads and quiet spaces. It felt like forever until we pulled into our parking spot at the top of the hill. He loved being outside, called it his "church," and I loved these mornings together.

The two of us would sit in our place, underneath the overhang with two long, old picnic benches and a stunning view of the lake. Some mornings a blanket of fog hovered over the water. We sat a table, Dad sitting so close next to me that I could smell his cologne. We never used many words. He didn't like to talk much, so I had to concentrate hard to make myself quieter. Dad spread out the paper and placed the milks out for us. I unrolled the bag, finally letting the sugariness into the air, and slowly reached for my éclair. I wanted to make it last, enjoying every bite and savoring every moment with Dad.

Donut times were my sacred times with Dad.

■　　■　　■

We stood there for a moment, my right of passage passing before us. For him, his youngest child was off to college. For me, freedom from the family drama. My mom and dad divorced when I was twelve: Dad left and Mom remarried. In the process I went to five different schools and bounced between homes. So I wanted to start my own life and find freedom to become the person I wanted to be, separate from the opinions and control of my family. In this moment of limbo, time was suspended as we both prepared to begin our own new chapters.

Dad took a deep breath and looked at me. I knew he was preparing to go, and the knot rose high in my throat. "Well, Lee-Wolfe," he said as he always did, my full name as one word, though this time with finality. "Here you are," he gestured to my miniature room. "I should get going. I love you." He reached over, hugged me warm and tight, and then kissed my cheek. His loving blue eyes warmed me and forced me to swallow. I didn't want to let him go.

■   ■   ■

In college I intended to find a Christian community like my Young Life group in high school, but the campus group that met in the gym was far from that. Way too serious. I actually found myself sitting next to a girl wearing a pink headband, so I fled after the last amen and didn't return.

Instead of seeking out other Christian groups for one that felt more comfortable, I joined a sorority and was soon elected class president. That became my spirituality as well as something else, something more harmful.

freshman fifteen

"Look who gained the freshman fifteen," a family member teased when I returned home after a few months of college. Those words were rooted with intentions of love, seeing a little girl who was so petite through high school finally growing into a woman. I know this now, but it was a punch in the stomach then.

What if I keep growing? What if the puffiness around my middle never stops? When I heard the words my mind decoded it like this: *You. Are. Fat.* Fat was not good. No, fat was bad. I would NOT be fat.

I stood in front of the full-length mirror in my dorm room and inspected the extra parts. These extra parts needed fixing—my stomach, my thighs, and those cheeks that were round and puffy, like two big apples on the side of my face. I would fix this. Fixing was my forte.

The cafeteria had rows of choices, from salads to pizzas, from cereal to sandwiches, with the ice cream station and the lines of desserts. Once I decided to start renovating the flaws, I walked in different, and it became overwhelming, like all of the food was screaming at me, "Eat me. Try me. Taste me!" *What is normal eating? What is healthy?* I had no plumb line on which to measure this. When I referred to the modeling of food behaviors by my own mother, it was extremes. All or nothing.

■　　■　　■

Slim and beautiful to my young eyes, she was a Farrah Fawcett look-alike. But my ears digested her discussions, discussions heard in far-away rooms. Talk of her weight gain. Her fat. Her diets.

The grapefruit diet. Sitting at the table with my plate piled high in colorful vegetables and juicy meat, hers contained only one oversized, pink grapefruit. Then the rice diet. Same scene, different meal: a bowl of white rice for her. Oftentimes it was a can of Slim-Fast. Treats, forbidden from her newest diets, were hidden. But there was a secret drawer to relieve her from the confines of dieting, which bulged with Oreos and chocolate cookies. Though there were rare times when she did have plates of meat and vegetables too, I was confused by them.

■　　■　　■

I received certain messages and interpreted them through my own lens like this:

Dieting? *Normal.*

Hating your body? *Normal.*

Thinness? *Search for it like the Holy Grail.*

Everyone dieted, right? Wasn't it a normal part of progression into womanhood?

The cafeteria began to swallow me up as I stood there, trying to decipher my needs. *What am I supposed to eat?* I had no idea, and a tiny voice whispered inside me, *Salad. Salad is safe. Stick with salad.* While nibbling the lettuce, I also began scanning the room like an FBI agent: *Who is eating what? Who is what size, and how can I do better than what they are doing? How can I lose this stupid layer of laziness that has attached itself to me?* I would fix it. I had no doubt I could. But I had no idea what a dangerous land mine I was walking into.

The fixing continued and I bought a scale. The scale held me, tipped over into the Land of Bad, a number in my head that I believed equaled fat. And the scale distorted my body into just a number, one that fueled my every action. By myopically focusing all my energy on my body, I was free from having to deal with any of the *real* emotional rumblings happening inside—those overwhelming feelings of sadness and lethargy, sprouting from a place I didn't understand and so ignored. The body was my diversion.

To overhaul my perceived fatness, I began to explore my options, and dieting seemed like the most logical choice. Dorm life was always filled with loads of food. I would just refrain from those foods that I (and the magazines I devoured for information) deemed bad. I had self-control. I could do it. Results were minimal. So I cut out more.

An encounter with chocolate cake seduced me further into the diet world. Down in the basement kitchen of my dorm, I created a succulent chocolate-frosted cake for a friend's birthday. I told myself it was a test. A test to see if I could actually resist the cake. *All* of the cake.

Sugar, flour, eggs, butter and the blender. No other thoughts but the cake. My nose was overtaken by the sweet, sugary confection whirling in the bowl. A voice, my own, bossy and determined, offering me this challenge above the blender's mixing sound: *Do not touch any of it to your lips.* I gazed longingly into the moist, yellow batter. My fingers secretly wanted to dip in and then touch my mouth for just one taste. Buds on my tongue were standing tall, waiting for relief. But I was stronger than this body of mine. I would control it despite the demands it inflicted on me. I was not going to succumb. Mean Lee's voice was firm, *Don't do it, Lee.*

And I didn't. Not a drop on that wanting finger, nor a lick of the spoon. I decorated and frosted the cake, graciously presenting it to my friend. A secret was planted.

voices

I was beginning to regret my decision of choosing this school in a Missouri town where nothing happened. Oftentimes the streets weren't even busy, and most of the students were commuters who went home on weekends.

I had a crazy roommate named Julia. She was short and had the sound of a squeaky toy. She had anxiety attacks and screamed a lot. Sometimes, to avoid her, I would skip the cafeteria altogether. Instead, I chose to eat a salad in my room with Jack and Jennifer on *Days of Our Lives*. I would also avoid Julia by going a block away to the football stadium, where I'd run the stairs, up and down the cement aisles. *Lose that weight, lose that weight*, I kept telling myself. *You don't want to be fat.*

I had read somewhere that I should remove fat from my diet. Since I was already freaking out about the college pounds, I thought this sounded like a nice, intellectual decision. This rationale was so popular, in fact, that you could find almost anything in the grocery store with the bold letters: **Fat Free**. So I started consuming as few things with fat as possible, or only items with the bold letters.

My friend Wendy from high school, who also came to school

with me, kept asking why I suddenly spent so much time working out. In truth, the exercise began to be the only thing that felt good, the only thing that gave me a feeling other than the dull grayness that was shadowing me. Wendy spent most of her time studying or with her boyfriend, Keith, who came to visit on the weekends. The highlight of my days was Jack and Jennifer on TV at 12:00 p.m., or my runs. I had auditioned for plays but wasn't cast in any of them. So I went to sorority functions but found the girls, who were mostly from the surrounding small towns, highly irritating. Even though I was in charge of events and connections, everything was losing its color.

I called my friend Dena at Kansas University. We spent hours on the phone—her telling fun stories of life in Kansas and me sharing bits and pieces of my life that wasn't cutting it. One day I was at a sorority function, standing near a gangly girl who never stopped talking, and she suddenly burst out, "You are my sister!" She ran over giddily and hugged me while I stood limp with my arms by my side. I already had a sister. I didn't even know this girl's name, and she was hugging me and calling me sister. By October I dropped out of the sorority and called Kansas University to see if I could transfer.

Tears from somewhere came often. I felt determined when I was working out or planning out my meals, but most other times, I was sad. I stopped journaling my feelings and stories, something I had done since I was seven years old. Now I only kept a journal of what I was eating and when, how much I was working out and when. Goals and measurements were always written all over the pages. Things that would make me feel some sort of success. Then I pushed it too far.

"What are you doing?" Wendy asked, her eyes fierce and stern as I came out of the bathroom stall.

I almost fell back at the shock of seeing her there with me. I thought I had been alone. Tears formed in her eyes as she continued to pound me with questions. "Lee? What are you doing? I heard you!"

I went to the sink to wash my hands. "I wasn't doing anything," I said.

"Yes, you were. I heard you throwing up! Why were you doing that?"

"I don't know. I just felt so gross after we ate all of that junk food. I had to get it out of me." I was so embarrassed and ashamed. I vowed to never do that again.

I wasn't comparing myself to anyone but me. I was the measuring stick. I was the person who wasn't measuring up to the person I was supposed to be, and I was angry about having all of these weird, uncomfortable emotions. *Where are they supposed to go? What is wrong with me?*

Shame had me feeling so rotten about myself, and it began to form into a voice, a voice that had been shaped from negative messages over the years that were buried deep. When I was strong and happy, I didn't hear the voice. But the more I began to tell myself I needed to work harder, telling myself I needed to eat less, it was as if a door opened and voices in different forms came in. They merged and swirled, and they became the voice of my measuring stick. Born out of voices from my past, of people who hurt me, of people whose words cut so deep that they now were my narrator in a life that wasn't playing out the way I wanted.

■　　■　　■

One of the voices that seeped back into my mind was from my dance line coach in high school. She always stood in fifth position, with her wiry arms on her hips, screaming at us. Looks of disgust. Eye rolls. And "Tsk tsks" from her tiny, wrinkled mouth, mostly aimed at me. She didn't like me.

When I was finally offered a lead role in the musical production at school, I was left with the choice of dance line or theater. I chose theater. She called me to her office, a tiny closet-like space near the locker room. "Hello Miss Lee, come in. Please shut the door behind you."

Nausea swept over me, mostly from looking at her wrinkly old skin, or possibly from the odor—a burnt smell of stagnant, dank air and her body overly cooked in a tanning bed, reeking of burnt skin. I sensed it wasn't a meeting to be filled with joy.

"I need you to explain to me this decision of yours?" she intoned.

I stared at her jet-black hair and her crinkly, long face. Years of dance and yelling lived in each of those lines. Her sadness and anger filled them. Her beady, black eyes rarely moved once she set her gaze on me. "I need to quit dance line," I said, not sensing a need to explain more.

The musty room suspended the silence above us. She stared unrelentingly at me. Her long, bony fingers crept to the edge of the desk where an apple sat. She put it in her hand and flipped her attention to it. My sweaty fingers clung to the sides of the chair.

"You see this apple, Miss Lee. This apple is shiny, red and beautiful. It is so appealing, isn't it? Miss Lee, you are just like this apple: beautiful on the outside, you appear to everyone that you are so good."

Slowly she turned the apple, and I saw the brown mushy spots. "Miss Lee, when you actually look at this apple and look inside, you will find it is rotten. You are just like this apple."

Her pruney lips curled into a smile while her arrow pierced into my heart. I didn't believe her then, thought she was cuckoo. But when darkness and clouds began to seep into my life, her voice returned.

■   ■   ■

Later in college I could hear that voice, "You are that apple, Lee. Don't you see?"

Had that been the only experience like this, maybe I would have stopped with my conclusion that she was crazy and let it go. But experiences like this had occurred more than once. I couldn't help but begin to ask questions, to inquire, to seek out an answer. *Maybe, maybe they were right?*

Locked in the bedroom of my great aunt's home in California, I was about nine years old. My parents had offered me an opportunity to stay with her for a few days: To feel like a big girl. To fly on a plane alone. The pilot came to meet me and gave me plastic wings. It was adventure at its best. I envisioned glamorous days at the pool and shopping in fancy stores with my great aunt.

Alcohol had another plan. Too much consumption sent Auntie sent into a rage during dinner at the long, mahogany table. Her words turned from soft to sharp. Her angry haze from too many gin-and-tonics forced me to run into the back bedroom, slamming and locking the door while her angry words pounded through the thick door. "You are the devil's child; don't you know that? So ungrateful to your parents. So rude. Not your brother, he would never act like you do, you evil child."

One sentence traps me into a future prison of words.

Petrified, the large, flowered paper walls suck me in. Collect phone call home: "Come get me. Auntie is saying mean things.

Come get me." I stayed there all night. Eyes wide. Heart racing. Flowers, ugly, large and colorful on every wall. No one came. They were used to the swings of alcohol and assured me it would all be better in the morning.

But the arrows pierced hard.

■   ■   ■

I wish I could say that, after I came home from that trip and explained to my parents what happened, that we had talked about it, that they had encouraged and reassured me that, "No, you aren't the devil's child. You aren't the accident." Instead it was brushed away, hidden beneath smiles. I needed something that wasn't offered to my little heart: Validation. Acknowledgment. Something, anything to help me process the cruelty of those words.

That year in college, while I was vulnerable and weak, those words returned to question me. Subtle at first, inquisitive, with questions like, *What if they are right? What if I am that person?*

When I began the rigidity of living my life based on food and numbers, these voices grew in my head. They grew with the family secrets, with the words I told myself over and over again: *You need to work harder, try harder, be better. This isn't like you, Lee, to be so lazy and undisciplined. What is wrong with you? Get it together.*

So I worked harder and harder. I began going home on weekends since there was nothing going on at school, but really I was going home for the aerobics. Body by Schlebe was a workout center that bred competition and comparison. Floor-to-ceiling mirrors, loud music pumping from every corner and a room packed with twenty-somethings, looking for crazy-hard workouts. This was serious aerobics, with high kicks, complicated dance sequences, and an instructor with a tiny waist, beautiful blond hair and not an ounce of fat on her body. I couldn't stop with one class and often I would stay for two. Kicking my legs higher than the girl next to me. Making sure I did one extra sit-up than the instructor. And then frantically working out on the Stairmaster before I left. Exercise wasn't for me but a way to be against me: to kick and push and squeeze the bad out of me.

Work harder, go longer, don't let anyone do it better, Lee. You must do this. Don't you want to be strong? Don't you want to be fit? Keep going. You can eat later; you can sleep later, the voice demanded and directed. But later never really came. It was as if the exercise would stop the thoughts for while. I had a reprieve when the endorphins kicked in, a place that was neutral and even. It left me light, and I liked light. I liked the grumbling in my tummy, the pain in my quads.

I transferred to Kansas University in Lawrence in January and left the emptiness of Missouri. I moved into the dorms on campus with my high school friends. But what was even more exciting was that Lawrence had a Body by Schlebe too.

5

renaissance

New school. New me. I knew the drill. I had been to five schools during elementary and junior high, and I had always told myself it was a clean slate and changing schools was a new adventure. Similarly, joining another sorority seemed like the only logical way to immerse myself in a community. I pledged a new sorority and was again elected class president. I joyfully moved into an enormous, white-pillared house full of college girls. Exercise was my respite from the zoo, with the onslaught of personalities and activity that constantly filled the house. Even if I also went to Body by Schlebe later, at the sorority house I could escape to the small back room that held a huge television, and early in the morning, in my stirrup pants and T-shirt, I would crunch and push to my Denise Austin fat-buster video. The scratchy voice coming from her gymnast-like body would tell me how great I was doing and how much harder I could work. I wanted stronger arms. I wanted a smaller tummy. I wanted to burn that fat.

Alive with activities and events, my social life was busy and fun. Not a single girl called me sister, so I stayed and sowed my oats, staying late most nights at a bar called Johnny's. I also began escaping the voices that followed me through pitchers of beer. In the back of my mind, something still nagged.

■   ■   ■

The year that I was twelve, Mom insisted the basement be refinished and hired a carpenter to complete the project: Joe. A skinny guy with curly, black hair and a wiry, black mustache. His jeans looked like someone poured baby powder on them, and he brought a smell of wood and sweat into any room he entered.

I heard him call out to my mom, "I need your input on something." I folded my arms into my chest and focused my eyes on the television where Smurfette ran from Gargamel. Behind me, I heard Mom follow Joe down the stairs with a little giggle. A giggle so quiet I might have missed it. But a giggle I knew. Like my sister Kristin's giggle when she was flirting on the phone with a boy.

I told myself I didn't hear a giggle. I told myself I was imagining it. I told myself it was hard to hear over Smurfette's high-pitched voice.

Later on, after Joe was gone each day and the Smurfs had ended, I would hear the sound of the garage door lifting. The familiar sound of Dad's car pulling in the garage awoke our new dog, Pepper, from her deep slumber. She wagged and flapped her tail on the carpet in excitement. The door opened and the gassy smell of garage blew into the living room. "Hey Pepper," he said cheerily as she ran to him. Pepper's dog collar rattled while he bent down to pet her, and seeing me in my chair he said, "Hi LeeWolfe!"

On those certain days I knew immediately. I could tell by the way he talked. It was in the slur of the words. Like when I painted with watercolors and had too much water, the colors

bled into one another, making the lines and the picture unrec-
ognizable. When I looked in his face I could see if it was there,
the red. His skin would turn bright tomato-colored red, illu-
minating his brilliant blue eyes, and I would turn in my chair
to see if the red was there. He crouched down, stroking Pepper's back with his hand, repeating, "Good dog, you are such a
good dog."

Daytime Dad was serious. Nighttime Dad laughed. The red
face set him free him from what he called, "Stresses of the job,
stresses of paying for this new house." At the same time, though,
red-faced Dad and his slurred words scared me. Scared me because I knew it made Mom angry. Mom didn't like this dif-
ference, but I did—sometimes.

I would hop out of my chair and run over to him when I saw
the red face, "Hi Daddy!"

He leaned down toward me, I threw my arms over his
shoulders, and he would give me a good squeeze. The smell of
Old Spice from the morning was now buried by cigarette smoke
and alcohol. Then he stood up and put his large hand on my
head, rustling my short hair. "How was your day?" he'd ask me.

"Good!" I told him about recess and band class and gym.
Told him about my friend Stacy and the new boy, Austin. He
took his coat off and threw it over the banister leading to the
basement that was under construction. I told him about the
school play. I told him about playing my trumpet. I told him
about everything I could think of as it fell out of my mouth.

He stopped on the carpet before the step up to the tiled
kitchen floor, and looked into me with his blue eyes, his smile
unveiling the small space between his two front teeth, "Wow,
LeeWolfe, sounds like you had a great day!"

On those days Mom knew too. She paid attention.

She was standing over the rust-colored stove, cooking dinner. Her shoulder-length, curly, blond hair rested neatly against her pretty, pink sweater, and her hand sat firmly on her left hip as she stirred something in a pot with her right hand. She didn't turn around when Dad entered the kitchen. I felt the mad in the air.

My hand in my pocket fiddled with a large piece of lint left from the wash, and the skin on my palms began to perspire. It felt like the time when I played hide-and-go-seek in the white, wicker hamper with the lid closed: the air siphoned away and everything still.

I watched him walk up to her, wrap his arms around her waist and kiss her neck. She stood stiff and didn't turn around. Her deep, low voice said, "You were at that Long Branch Bar again."

I took that as my signal to retreat from the coming cloud that was preparing to touch down in the kitchen. I called Pepper, "Come here girl," and lured her upstairs into my bedroom to play.

On nights when Dad visited the Long Branch and after we were tucked in our beds, the winds picked up in our house, doors slammed and loud voices traveled up through the vents into our bedrooms. On these nights I would lie still in my pretty, flowered-wallpapered bedroom trying to lose myself in my little black-and-white TV. Episodes of *Hart to Hart* and *Fantasy Island* helped me go to sleep and drown out the fighting.

My brother, Corky, was usually so tired from soccer that I wondered if he even heard them, while Kristin was habitually talking on the phone or playing her record player. I knew she heard it. It had to bug her too, didn't it? I wondered but never asked.

One night, I couldn't take the yelling and fighting, so I quietly tiptoed down the carpeted stairs, holding my breath. I walked into the vortex of a storm not caused by weather but by people.

People who were supposed to love each other.

I slipped into the living room, telling myself not to be afraid. Dad was by the fireplace, his buttoned shirt untucked, his tie gone, and his short glass filled with ice and a brown drink in his hand. Mom was on the couch, her head in her hands. I walked behind the couch and sucked in my breath: "Stop fighting!" I said loudly so they both could hear. "Be nice to each other!"

I shocked them and, for what felt like ten minutes, no one moved. Dad looked at me, but I am not sure he really saw me, perhaps looking beyond me. Mom lifted her head from her hands and then slowly turned her head. The color on her face vanished as she saw me standing, in my Garfield nightgown, in the middle of their storm. Her eyes with black mascara speckled underneath them looked at me like she wished she didn't see me standing there.

I too began to wish that I wasn't there but hidden away in my room. She moved over to me and knelt down to where my body stood. Her blue eyes were encircled by red. "Oh, Sunshine," she said quietly. "Daddy and I aren't fighting; we are just talking loudly. Adults do that sometimes." She tried to smile, but it was the kind of smile made for cameras and clerks at the grocery store. It wasn't the happy-mom smile.

I couldn't hug her back. My arms were glued to my side, next to the polyester itch of my nightgown. I wanted to yell, "I am not five years old! I know what is going on around here, and I hear your fighting!" But I said nothing.

They divorced later that year.

■   ■   ■

Now in college, I was flirting with the alcohol to see if it would bite me. But it only left me with terrible guilt, another measuring stick that said I wasn't measuring up. Now I wasn't measuring up for God. Here I was, calling myself a Christian. I was a hypocrite. I told God that I would come back to him, but right now I just wanted to play. I wanted success and measurable things.

Even at a new school, the pressure and the drive in my head came with me. It came with me in the basement of the sorority house at meals. No more cafeteria but sit-down, family-style eating. My eyes watched to see what the girls ate, and my allowance of food was always less. With so many women in one house, it was a constant battle of comparisons. And then my world switched into overdrive.

"You can't major in theater and broadcast news!" the college guidance counselor said one day when I was sought advice on registering for spring classes. He looked down at me with his glasses on his nose, laughing.

"Why not?" I said.

Both were intense majors, requiring full commitment. But I was determined. Each day, despite how late I stayed out at a sorority party or Johnny's, I would be up early, briskly walking to campus for an over-full day in two separate buildings. Breakfast was no longer incorporated in my busy schedule, so my pockets were filled with cereal. My hands offered my mouth only little bites of food between classes. Any other time I would be drinking Diet Coke.

I can handle it, I told myself while existing on fumes. I was either a renaissance woman, or I was stupid.

I wrote my news stories and memorized my sonnets. And I would walk back and forth, back and forth, up the hills and down the hills, from the world of suits and intensity in the journalism building to the world of creativity in the lively theater hall.

And then there was the other problem. The theater world was not friendly to me showing up with bold Greek letters emblazoned on my sweatshirts. They didn't want to hear about my latest date dash or the sorority drama in the house. Similarly, my sorority sisters didn't want to hear about how much Shakespeare I was memorizing, or how deep and intricate the thoughts were behind the character in the latest play. And my Christian friends, how would I tell them about my many, many nights drinking at Johnny's?

With my cereal in my pocket and my Diet Coke in my hand, my legs pushed me up and down the steep stone stairs. I was like a rat on a wheel, just spinning. Trying to prove something. I didn't have time to feel, didn't have time to eat. I pushed and listened to the voice telling me to prove it. I could hear the college counselor's words, eerily echoing in my head, now a part of the chorus of voices I was fighting that were pushing me harder and harder.

I focused on these goals and the outside. I didn't have to pay attention to the inside. Because whatever was inside, I couldn't fix. Yet, the tug and pull of emotions was washing me over— despite the new college, a gaggle of fun and loving friends, and even plenty of dates. *Who was I? Where did I belong?*

whispered prayer

Mom had married Joe, the carpenter, when I was in seventh grade, and they bought an old blue house with a detached garage. She pushed me to like Joe, but nothing about him made him huggable to me—not his flannel, plaid work shirts, his wire mustache or his fancy Cadillac that took up too much space in our garage.

Nevertheless, despite my anger at his intrusion in our lives and Mom's need to force me to like him, he became my buddy. We would watch TV shows together, he helped me with my homework, and he even taught me how to make a really good Spam dinner. We also bickered often, as his stubbornness was just about equal to mine.

I had feared when he entered our lives that he would take the place of Dad, but that wasn't the case as my heart held him in another place—a place of endearment made for a good step-father. The years in the blue house I was mostly with Joe, and he grew to be someone special. Kristin and Corky were off at college, and Mom was often traveling with her job and her business partner, Ron. So Joe, kindhearted and caring, was my fashion police whenever I was home from school.

"How does this look?" I would ask him while he stretched out on the couch, me standing in front of the large TV.

"Good."

"No, I don't believe you. Come on; look at the back. How does it look in the back?"

"Good."

"Okay, so really good? Or just okay good?" I would say with my arms spread out wide. "Tell the truth. I don't want to look like a dork. Which outfit do you like better?"

"I like that one. It looks cute," he would say with a smirk, knowing I hated the word *cute*.

The summer before junior year was the last, and worst, summer I spent at home. I had moved out of the main house to a little apartment over the garage, and I painted it a bold pink, stenciling wolves on the borders of the walls. Protecting me from the world, this pink room with my wolves was my personal retreat—though it lacked a bathroom and a kitchen so I had to use the house for basic needs.

Mom and Joe had been married about seven years when the unsettledness began, during this summer that I lived with wolves in my pink room. I knew the feeling every time I entered the house through the antique wood door and into the large kitchen, with the sun heating the beautiful maple cabinets Joe had made. Mom was being secretive. Her extra-long tanning appointments. Her stuttering words in response to questions about where she was going. Her eyes darting away when talking to me. It didn't take a rocket scientist to know that people don't go tanning for two hours, that whispering and giggling on the phone doesn't happen with girlfriends, and that her excessive travel with her "business partner" was much more. I knew. And I couldn't mind my own business.

One evening while both of us were home, we found ourselves on the narrow, wooden staircase nestled between the dining and TV rooms. I sat on the third stair up, and she stood, leaning against the banister. Her blond hair was freshly cut short with fun, soft curls wiggling this way and that. *She has such great style,* I thought to myself. However, her flowery perfume choice that had once drawn me to her now clogged the air between us. I stopped her as she was making her way to her bedroom, ready to dissect to the root—the root of truth. The truth about the evasiveness. The truth about the darty eyes and the long tanning sessions. I knew the answer, knew it in my gut, but I wanted her to admit it.

"Mom," I said, no longer bold. I was afraid. "I need to ask you something."

My insides tightened. Thoughts ran around in my head. I let them run with their doubts, their fears and their insecurities. They scattered about, and I focused. I was not going to be deferred from asking this question.

I looked at her, and her lips were gathered at one side of her face. She was biting her bottom lip like she does when she is thinking, and her pretty blue eyes stared down at me, her child.

I gathered my breath, waved away the thoughts and said, "Mom, I am only going to ask you this once."

We locked eyes. Blue on blue. Mother on daughter. Daughter on mother.

"And I want you to know, if you lie to me, I will never, ever forgive you." I trembled, suddenly becoming cold.

Her eyes widened. Her lips pursed. She squinted at me.

"Are you having an affair with Ron?"

■　　■　　■

Christmas break earlier that year, before the house changed, I came home to make money. Waitressing filled my pockets with cash, and I also helped Mom out in her office at the apparel mart for more money. Her space was one of many boxlike rooms in the wings of a large arena. When the market was open, the arena was alive with thousands of people and clothing booths.

Mom's office stood apart from the rest of the rooms, with her design skills reflected in every detail: colorful curtains on the dull glass doors, and light pinks and shades of greens brightened her walls. In the back of the room were her files and a small white desk. While her decorating skills exceeded most, her organizational skills were less exemplary.

I spent my time there in the back, labeling, sorting, tossing and organizing. Cleaning up her piles and the little messes she left behind. Now I tried to patch up the places where she made holes.

She had a childlike flutter that Christmas. I wondered if it was just a creative spark or a boost in business, but something new was happening with her.

One day, I sat at the desk, my hands deep in paperwork, and noticed the unsettled feeling. I was unsure why at first. *Don't I want my own mother to be happy? Don't I care about her and her desires to live a good life?* I asked myself. Yet something signaled fear and distrust. The voice hidden just under the surface reprimanded my fears, telling me to be a nice daughter and stop being so judgmental.

But I sensed something.

Mom's business partner, Ron, appeared. He was tall, thin and balding. He walked with long strides, and his back was straight as a board. He was overconfident and arrogant with a tan face and lines circling his lips from too many cigarettes.

They sat down at the round table, looking at large books of inventory.

This wasn't my first meeting with Ron. He had been around here and there, but I stayed out of his way. I had my own opinion about him, different from Mom's gushing about how helpful he had been with her business.

I pulled out manila file folders and tried to ignore him, except out of the corner of my eye. The chairs. Their chairs. Why were they so close to each other? Too close.

Stop it, Lee. Stop it, the voice said.

Conversation continued, lively and giggly. I knew that giggle from the stairs of my house—when a carpenter interrupted our lives. A carpenter I was now protective of. One I trusted and loved.

Ron coughed a gross, smoker cough, forcing all the phlegm out of his lungs. I lifted my head, and under my breath, mumbled, "You shouldn't smoke all of those cigarettes."

Mom threw a have-some-tact-young-lady smile at me, and they continued their work. She was too polite. Too sweet. Not herself. Normally she would have lectured me right then about my bad manners, but she didn't. I knew what was going on, but I told myself I was wrong and scolded myself for the thoughts. *Ignore it; push it down. Don't feel it. Don't talk about it. Not my business. Not my life. Why do I care?*

■　　■　　■

Christmas Eve.

My sister and I showed up to the fancy restaurant Mom had made it a tradition to eat at. We had learned over the years how important it was to behave on holidays, the lecture so often directed at me. "It is Christmas, and I spent all of this time and money on you! The least you can do is beeeehave," she would yell in her southern drawl, eyes narrowed in a you-make-me-so-embarrassed look. Holidays always warranted our best behavior.

So we acted the polite, sweet daughters who showed up when she told us to. The restaurant was dark and filled with little old men who could have been mistaken for members of the mafia. Kristin and I walked up to the hostess station, spotting Mom at the table in the back. She had someone with her. But it wasn't Joe. It was Ron. He eyed us and quickly got up, his long, stringy legs moving toward us. He hugged us, leaving us with a cheap-cologned kiss on the cheek. I wanted to gag. I pulled back, away from him.

"Can I talk to you girls outside?" Ron said quickly.

"Sure," Kristin responded. Always so polite, my older sister—so willing to do what she needed to do to keep peace.

I bit my tongue when I really wanted to lash at him. I didn't like him, and I sensed something untrustworthy in him.

Outside, the daylight blinded our eyes. "I received a call today from your grandmother," he said. His eyes feigned sympathy, "Your Great-Aunt Katherine took a fall last night and died."

My chest tightened and my shoulders curled in. I clenched my jaw and furrowed my brow. I swallowed to take it down. I should have cried. I didn't.

I looked at my sister, who had tears in her eyes. My sister was closer with my great-aunt than I was. She was always one to look beyond the bad, or maybe just ignore the bad.

I felt guilty for not crying. The voice growing in my head told me how selfish I was to lack emotion for her death. But she was mean. Mom loved her deeply, despite her verbal lashings, she loved her. She looked past her unlikability, but I couldn't.

Kristin and Ron discussed how to handle the situation, and

apparently decided to have lunch as planned and act as if nothing happened.

The "nothing-happened game." One I learned to be really good at.

When Kristin and I left, Ron would give Mom the news. "Why ruin Christmas Eve dinner?" he said.

It is already ruined with you here, I wanted to say.

The three of us walked back into the restaurant and played the game. Kristin and I were sweet and polite, asking Ron about his kids, asking the two of them about work. We smiled and laughed at the right times, and listened to smoky Ron talk. I ordered salad with dressing on the side. While feigning interest in Ron and working hard to ignore the relationship between the two of them, I busied my hands and my mind by cutting the salad into little bites. I wanted the lettuce to last throughout the entire lunch.

I counted each bite while I chewed. One, two, three, four, five, six, swallow.

Focus and count, focus and count. Don't listen to the thoughts in your head, Lee. Focus and count.

Why am I having lunch with this man? I wondered.

Where is Joe?

Aunt Katherine is dead.

Aunt Katherine had many more drunken rages after the time I was alone with her. Her words to me, "You selfish little girl; you spoiled little brat." Her tiny little body, her wrinkly old face, sitting in her old chair, with her long fingers gripping tightly to her cocktail. Mom had sat on the couch, calmly. Politely. Not arguing. "Smile," Mom would say. "She is old. She doesn't know what she is doing."

Counting. Salad.

Distracting me from feeling.

Helping me escape.

Chew, one, two, three, four, swallow.

Chew, one, two, three, four, swallow.

I was away from what was actually happening. Away from the present. Away from the truth. The truth, not allowed to be spoken. The games and the daughters so polite and well-mannered, playing their parts.

Chew, one, two, three, four, swallow.

We smiled. And we buried it deep.

■   ■   ■

Right there on the thin, old staircase, I couldn't hold it in anymore. It was eating me up inside. And now it was out. No more whispers on phones and secret meetings, but real words putting a name on it. Sitting in the heat between the two of us, waiting for one of us to grab the words and do something with them. Suspended in air.

I looked at her, and she looked away, past me. She didn't see the hurt it caused me. But I also didn't see it. I didn't see her and her need to be loved, to be cherished, to be filled. A need, strangely similar to my own, that I was beginning to fill with games around food. Both of us, needing each other and God. Both of us soul-hungry. Mother and daughter seeking, lacking, wanting. And we didn't connect, but hurt and wounded each other.

She answered, and I sucked in one last breath of hope that she might confide in me, might tell me the truth.

"No, Lee," she said sarcastically. "Ron and I are not having an affair."

So I had my answer, though I knew the real answer. And I was, again, to keep quiet. She couldn't tell me the truth. To offer me the truth would mean turning the mirror on herself, taking a look at the patterns. She lightly hugged me and the conversation was over as she quickly walked out.

Brush, brush, under the rug yet again.

I sat on the wooden stair. Salt tears burned my face.

The voice returned. It didn't allow me to sit and feel the pain, but shamed me: *You are too sensitive. You think too much.*

I heard the voice and I heard me.

I heard me say, "She is lying. And she looked me right in the eye and lied to me!"

The voice said, *You are in her way, always in the way of her getting what she wants. The accident.*

This voice and my voice began to become one.

I felt like I didn't matter to her enough for her to tell me the truth. *At twenty-one, couldn't I handle the truth?* Pain. Dark, thick pain swirled the walls of the lining in my stomach.

I whisper a prayer that would torment me for many, many years: "God, I wish Ron were dead. I wish he would just die."

florida

The divorce stipulations had sent me back and forth between Mom's and Dad's, so Dad moved into a condo about a mile away from Mom, making the transition easier. However, the back and forth wasn't only in the driving but also in the games they played: Mom probing me for stories about Dad and his life. Dad and his snide comments about Mom and her life. Checks handed to me in envelopes by Dad for my living provided by Mom.

I was like silly putty, molded and shaped, squished and pulled between the tension of the two homes. But I also used it to my advantage—running to Dad's when Mom and I fought, and running to Mom's when I'd had enough of Dad. I played into the games for my benefit. After the stairs confrontation, I ran away to Dad's—but only after leaving Mom a note informing her I would not be her travel partner to visit my grandfather in Florida. As the only child left at home in the summers and not paying my own rent, there were still expectations of me. The idea of spending days with Mom in the car after our previous encounter sounded like hell.

The phone rang and I heard Dad call upstairs to me. I picked up the plastic, white phone with the springy cord on the bed stand. This is how these conversations went: Mom, screaming at me for how selfish I was. Me, feeling guilty in knowing I ran to Dad's for safety. Repeated words, "You are so selfish! How dare you do this to me?"

This time I did scream back at her. "I don't want to go with you to Florida. You can't make me go. Why can't I make my own decisions? I am twenty-one years old."

"I am your mother, and you will do what I say! Do you hear me?"

I succumbed. Mostly out of guilt. Maybe out of a tiny hope that the relationship could be repaired. Or possibly out of an insane need to prove I wasn't the selfish daughter she said I was.

Off to Florida we went. Me, Mom, and the lies and secrets. I slapped a smile on my face. I was expected to do this, to smile and act like a lady. And I did. I did because a voice in my head screamed, "All I have done for you! The least you can do is go on this trip with me!" Or her other famous line, "I am your mother. Someday I will be dead and you will regret this."

Joe let us borrow his fancy, black Cadillac for the trip. The car, with its cream leather interior and a brand-new smell, Mom drove like it is was a Corvette. Diet Coke in her right hand, her left holding the leather wheel, and fifties music blared through the speakers.

"Isn't this going to be fun?" she squealed with a smile. No memory of the previous day's fight existed. Everything was fine. I tried to tell myself that, but my body didn't buy it. It smelled fear. The car reeked of her sweet perfume. She reached down into the console to grab a handful of jellybeans. Must be a new diet.

I was riding on hope for something more, for a place on the other side of the anger where we could talk calmly, where feelings could be expressed and validated, and where different opinions and views were accepted. I was hoping for something that didn't happen in this family. I didn't know I had to look elsewhere, beyond them. I needed the same love and approval that my mother was still searching for from her own family. Both of us were coming up empty when we had the capacity to offer it to the other.

I needed a lifeline to hang onto during the never-ending drive, so I prayed silently over the chatter in my mind. I asked God for help. Asked for help in getting through this. But the feelings of wanting to escape were so enormous I wondered if he could help. Did I trust him? Or did he agree with her? *How do I know, my years in this life so few, maybe she is right? Maybe I need to take a look at myself and discover my own brokenness and not pin everything at her,* I wrote in my journal. Maybe, but right then I just wanted to escape from her smiling face, singing loudly to her moronic music and pretending nothing was wrong.

I found my escape. I found it in every meal I ate with her. I made sure to eat less than her, made sure not to fill myself with too much food, made sure to protect myself from too much feeling. If she was not going to protect me, then I would find my own way. The hunger pains comforted me. A twisted way to punish myself, not allowing myself too much fullness. Fullness began to mean feeling, and I didn't want to feel.

After two days of travel and little food, my head felt lighter. Like the laughing gas they give you at the dentist's office, my head was wobbly and airy. Thoughts begin to slow down and the bubbling inside dissipated. The need for food and my strength to not eat the food became the constant thoughts in my head. I had my drug; I had my way to numb out.

We arrived in Naples, Florida, late in the evening. We were

staying at my grandfather's stepdaughter's apartment. Grandpa was called Pop Pop. He divorced my grandma after my mom's sister died of leukemia. Mom was left without any other siblings. Her own parents were traumatized by the death, and in my opinion, took their anger out on Mom. Who now took it out on me.

Mom and I walked up the long steps into the apartment on the second floor. We were bombarded when we opened the door: orange walls, yellow wicker furniture, yellow flowered curtains. Everywhere you turned were framed pictures of people in space, people with hands lifted toward the stars, and crystals hanging from the ceiling. The place smelled of incense and weed.

I didn't care. I was exhausted. I stumbled to the yellow bathroom and began washing my face. I heard Mom in the other room. She had the portable phone and escaped outside onto the porch. The sliding glass doors closed, and her southern laugh came through the doors and pierced my ears. I scrubbed my face hard. I threw the hot water into my eyes again and again. I knew she wasn't calling Joe. She would have called him inside. Did she really think I didn't see? That I didn't know? Did she really think I was that naive? I knew she was calling Ron. I knew that laugh.

I finished washing my face, brushed my teeth and walked back into the room, ready for bed. My body cold, my head spinning, I wrapped myself alone in the comforter and closed my eyes to shut out the day.

The next day, I announced, "I am going on a run" after the breakfast dishes were cleared. I couldn't get out of the house fast enough. To run. To run away, my legs moving fast, the anxiety coming out of me as I fled away from the house, down the street of one-story Florida homes. I paid no attention to anything around me except my feet moving fast. Away.

I hated her.

I hated him.

I hated that I hated her. I hated that we couldn't talk about this.

I hated myself for whispering that prayer. Wishing Ron was dead.

What about me? Am I going to be just like her? Am I a liar too? Will I ever be different from her, do I have the ability to be authentic and honest with myself and others?

Alone. The overwhelming feeling there was alone. I didn't feel God. I didn't feel me. I just felt running and running fast.

Far away from Pop Pop's house, I ran into a town. Then past a waterway filled with boats and then past one-story yellow homes with white Cadillacs in the driveways. I ran and my breath kept up with me. My arms and legs moved to the speed of my mind. For the first time in two days I felt free. Free from her. Free from the chains holding me down. Free.

And then a sadness came. A sadness for her. As much as I was angry at her, I was sad for her too. For her life and what it was like for her to lose her only sibling. To be left alone, with no one's hand to hold onto. No one to comfort her as her own parents' grief tore them apart. How much could be expected from her with all she had been through? How lonely she must have been. And her mother now, who continued to talk about the daughter in the grave, as if she was the angel. And my Mom, always chasing her shadow to prove *she* was good enough. She was the child that lived.

Did anyone see her? I hated her and I loved her, and the tension was so hard to sort through. I saw Mom like I have never seen her before. And I understood, for the first time, her hurt inside. She was doing the best she could, wasn't she? Even if her best didn't come close to what I needed from her. My heart was aching now. I wanted to be there for her. Yet I was so angry by the scars left on me. Sorrow and conflict ripped at me.

Both of us lost and hurting in broken families, longing for a family that was whole.

I turned down a street similar to Pop Pop's with a waterway in the alley and bright-colored, long cars in the driveways. Raindrops began to fall on my head, and the saltwater smell was thick in the air. I kept running and it rained harder. I sobbed. I ran. And in all of this, I realized I had no idea where I was.

I was completely lost.

Every street I turned onto looked the same. My heart beat fast. Arms stiffened as they pumped through the thick air. The winds began to blow and whip at me. My gray T-shirt was heavy with water. I stopped. I leaned over and placed my hands on my thighs to steady my shaking body. Rumblings of tears and shaking. My heart contracted tight. My breathing rapid.

I was lost and I was having my first real panic attack.

Hands trembled. Heart beat out of my chest. I walked and prayed out loud through my tears, "Please, God. Help me find my way back." A prayer for more than finding my way back to my grandfather's home, but my way back to life, to God, my way back to the person he created me to be. Was I looking for a way back or a way out? "Please, God. Help me find my way out of this maze of pain," I prayed over and over.

"God, please help me. God, please help me."

Hazed. Confused and dazed. I looked up and found myself in front of my grandfather's house. I had made it back safely—with no idea how. But I had. I stopped and sat on the curb, catching my breath that left me for so long, and brought it back to me.

Later on, we were eating in a diner. I could sense that Mom was desperate for her father to wrap her into an embrace of approval. To bless.

But Pop Pop was duplicitous in his behaviors. More of a circus clown in my memory than a grandfather, he also had a dark side—a stark contrast to the jokester of my childhood. On that day in the diner, there were no knock-knock jokes or battery-operated toys. The waitress sauntered over to take our order, and then Mom excused herself to go to the restroom. I felt him staring at me with his light eyes. They narrowed in on me like a cat ready to pounce on its prey. He set his cigarette down in the glass tray. I stayed quiet, wanting to fold myself into an envelope and fly away. I looked up, crossed my legs and stuffed my hands tight between. Fear.

He spoke at me in his smoker's voice and leaned forward to make sure I heard, "The way you are treating your mother is rude and selfish."

My hands trembled. I looked back into him as hard as he was looking at me. I would not run away in fear. I would not bow my head and pretend I didn't hear.

"You have no idea what I have been through, the lies, the deceit . . ." I say, but the words melt away with the smoky air— meaningless, misunderstood.

I sputtered something else, but it only was in my mind, not in my words. The swirling words of the little girl inside, asking, "New fathers, new houses, new schools, new lies, new secrets. Does anyone care what it has been like for me?" I wanted to yell in his wrinkly, old face, but I didn't because I felt an anger in him that could hurt me.

Motivated by my lack of compliance, he continued. "You are such a selfish little brat, treating your mother the way you do. The things you say to her, your attitude, all she has done for you. The least you can do is be nice to her. Someday you will regret the way you are treating her!"

I felt those arrows slaughter me. I tightened my lips and ground my teeth hard. My body was stiff and tense when Mom returned and slid into the booth. I wanted to shrink away like Alice in Wonderland. To fall deep in the hole and never return. To go away. I wasn't there anymore. They didn't see me.

That was the last time I ever saw or spoke to my grandfather. He died shortly after that trip.

8

numb

The voices were all swirled up and mixed together, so I obeyed the ones that kept me moving. Kept me running, literally running from my insides that were so twisted. What was the point of feeling? What was the point of allowing the feelings? What good would they do me? And if they washed over me, if I really let them out and allowed them to suck me up like I thought they would, would I really live through it? Or would I become a sad, lonely woman, complaining about the family that didn't give her what she needed or wanted? Ludicrous. Many people have hard lives. *Who cares?* I wondered. The only way I could see was forward. And I would move forward. Until a phone call knocked me down hard.

While I was back at school, attempting to be Superwoman, preparing for my sorority's rush and the start of my junior year, my sister called. I was sleeping at my friend Jen's house—we'd gone to high school together—on her blue futon. I had come to school early to get out of the house of lies and to perform in our sorority's rush skits. I was relieved to be back in my own life, ready to make it better than those who seemed to be ruining it for me. Deep in the thickness of my dreams, Jen frantically called my name, "Lee! Lee?" She was next to me in a long T-shirt, "Your sister is on the phone."

Late-night phone calls only meant something was wrong. Before Jen handed me the phone, I thought of every possible disaster that included my loved ones. Fearfully I spoke into the white cordless phone, "Hello?"

"Lee," said Kristin, my sweet sister, the dutiful one always making the calls when the family needed her to. "Ron died."

"Oh," I said, feeling a bit of relief that it wasn't Mom or Dad who died. "What happened?"

"He had a heart attack. While he and Mom were on a business trip. She found him dead on the floor of the bathroom. She is pretty shaken up . . ." Kristin kept talking matter-of-factly. I stopped listening and only heard, "Ron is dead. Mom needs you. Can you come home?"

I didn't want to come home. I was happy to be away from home. *You selfish little brat. All you think about is yourself.* The quicksand of words, and the confusion about how to feel. Why wasn't I sad? *You wished this, remember?* Those words stared down at me. I wasn't sad for Ron's death. And I wondered how I could not be sad for the loss of a life. *What is wrong with me? Am I really that self-centered?* I was sad for Mom—another tragedy for her to endure. But what about the scene? I thought of the scene, and that turned the sad into blood-boiling, fueling angry.

Dead in a hotel room with Mom.

Did my sister hear that? Did she care? I wanted to throw that futon out the window. I wanted to run through the streets screaming. And then I wanted to hit and hurt me. Me, the one who whispered that prayer. I didn't know how to hurt myself, except to let the voices loose. And to not allow myself any sort of pleasure. I didn't deserve that kind of pleasure: me the one

who loves God but wishes people dead. I had spoken those
words out loud; I had wished his death. *Cruel.*

I went home.

Like a good daughter, I missed the week of rush. I played the
role. I knew how to play it. Mom was happy to have me home
and hugged me tightly when I arrived in the blue house where
she lived with Joe. The woman who lost her lover. The lines
under her eyes filled with mascara, and the lipstick faded into
the wrinkles of her lips. Her face pale, she exuded grief. And
Joe. Where was Joe? Did Joe know? I don't know where he was,
but he wasn't living in the house anymore. I shoved down and
pushed away my feelings. I helped. I cleaned up. I smiled and
hugged and comforted. I kept quiet. I felt nothing but the voice
demanding me not to eat. Demanding me to be the dutiful
daughter. Demanding my servitude to the situation.

Like Mom's little ducklings, we were lined up next to her in
the pew. Dressed nicely in our funeral wear, the three of us sat
next to her. The church's stained-glass windows colored the air
with reds and blues. The center cross stared down over the
casket and the altar. It whispered to me, *Devil's child.* The cross
did not comfort me. It shamed me. It stared at me and made me
turn away in utter disgust at myself. It reminded me of my hor-
ribleness in wishing him dead. It screamed sin. I was the sinner.

Pictures of Ron and his children hung neatly from poster-
boards on easels. My eyes circled the mahogany casket. I spotted
other photos between the family photos.

Photos of Mom and Ron.

Mom and Ron by the lake. Mom and Ron with their arms
around each other. Mom and Ron smiling happily.

Into the colors and through the windows my eyes went, and
my mind spun up and disappeared. I wanted to fly away on one

of the sweet angel's wings, beautifully detailed in the etching on the glass. While I was there, flying into the distance, the shell of me sat on the hard wooden pew in my black dress that hung on my disappearing body.

My face wore the look of mourning.

My inside was empty.

I kept the stomach empty because it didn't deserve to feel full. It began to growl and speak at me. I ignored it. I was flying with white cotton wings, and I ignored its wants and desires. The numbness helped and soothed. It provided a light emptiness in my head. I liked the lightness. I liked the empty. I liked the space where empty was left with no thoughts but a simple hum.

That hum became my drug.

I pined after that feeling of flying and lightness, the feeling of shrinking. I didn't fill the stomach. *Too much,* the voice would tell me. *Too much. You are too much.* So I stayed in that place where the head was light and the eyes saw stars. *That will keep you safe. That will protect you,* the voice promised. I listened and obeyed.

They told stories of Ron. Nice tears and laughter flowed through the room while strangers spoke fondly of him. All I could smell was smoke. No one was smoking, but it smelled of smoke. Like he was there, sitting near us. His smoky smell. His phlegmy cough. We followed Mom dutifully out of the church where arms and bodies hugged me, touched me, wrapped me. People I didn't know. People who didn't know me. I didn't want their touch. I didn't want their looks. Sad people. I wasn't sad. I was furious. I shivered at the touching, shivered at the looking and the "I am so sorry" platitudes. And I stayed in my land of numb, where skin can't feel and words can't hurt. Where I could behave and not be too much.

Back in the kitchen, among the cabinets Joe built, I served food to the grieving. I didn't touch any of it. I served as people came in and out of my house. My backyard. My kitchen. Some sat crying, some laughed, all remembered and mourned Ron. All but me.

Death can be an opportunity to wake you up, to live life more fully. Death paralyzed me—the me buried inside—asleep in a life I was too afraid of.

9

hungry

I returned to college hungry after Ron's death. I was hungry not only physically but also spiritually. I found plenty to fill the hole. To stop and breathe meant I had to feel. I dove into it all: college, sorority life and as much social life as I could find. The voice bossed me around to move forward and do more: *No one wants to hear about your pain.* So I didn't talk about it. The more I busied myself the less time I had to eat. And the less I ate, the less I had to feel. A new way of life was now my normal. One where the voice made eating a game—the game of eating less then those I was with, of running farther than this girl or that girl. My sorority sisters complimented me, "You are so self-controlled. You look so great! I wish I could be as disciplined as you." The compliments and the constant striving fueled me and filled the aching place inside me, the hunger in my soul.

I found another distraction in a handsome frat boy named Ryan. We met at a party early in the year, him standing long with an old leather cowboy hat resting on his head. His light eyes so clear and tender. I was enveloped into him from the moment I first saw him.

He pulled in front of my sorority house in his brand-new,

green Ford Explorer. He was the ideal everything for me because he and I looked good together. "Such a cute couple," people would say. Looks were important; I knew this early on. When we talked back, Mom often said, "Don't be so ugly!" I would not be ugly, and he wasn't anywhere close. Ryan looked fresh out of a J.Crew catalog, and we spent months going to parties and formals. I was distracted by him—in a good way. He helped me feel alive when I was working hard to disappear.

I stepped into his car and leaned over to kiss his cheek. The stubble was fresh, and I smelled the worn leather from his shoes. My stomach was fluttery and empty. With him around, I couldn't help but feel. Feelings all over in my tingly toes, my pounding heart and my sweaty palms. I was persistently working to numb myself out, and he was continually waking me up. There was tender kissing and gentle caressing. His warm, large hand holding my neck while his soft lips connected me to him. I melted into him. Almost. Except for the part that wouldn't budge. The part filled with fear. What if he saw the real me? The bad-apple me. He was evoking so much life in the body I was trying so hard to ignore. This person here in this car, being loved by someone. How could he like this person? This person once faithful to God? This person who wished death on another and sat tearless to watch dirt tossed over a deathbed? Would he run away when he saw the truth?

Easy solution. Don't tell him the truth.

I didn't tell him much about my family, my pain or my struggle to fill my stomach. I smiled and loved him and didn't get too close. It didn't work.

The mad pace continued for me—only now any free time I had was spent with him. My double major was also working, mostly. I went to audition for the lead role in *Gypsy*. I stood on the stage, belting out the words, "Let me entertain you. Let me make you smile." My hands fluttered around, my feet in a sweet tap, until I tripped on the lip of the stage and fell into the lower portion. My mind wasn't as sharp, and my body wasn't as quick due to my lack of nutrition. I just wrote it off as a bad audition.

Ryan valued fashion and good looks, so I became very aware of making sure my outfits were just right, as well as my looks. If I focused on the outside, I didn't have to think about the inside.

I stopped by his fraternity house to see him after a run one day, my body covered in sweat and my T-shirt clinging. Ryan looked at me with eyes of desire and interest. "I love that you run," he said when he saw me. "You are starting to look like those girls on *90210!*"

He pulled me to him, his compliment well-meaning. His heart beating strong next to mine. But it stayed with me as another measuring stick, as if that was how I must be because that was how he wanted me to be.

Later on, in the spring, I walked down the hall of my sorority house and past the couch where some of my sorority sisters were lounging, watching the enormous TV.

I saw it in their eyes.

Suddenly, it was as if I had some sort of disease. They no longer complimented; now they stared when I walked by. They tried to hide the stares, but I could feel them all over me as I walked. I felt the cold looks on my behind, my arms, my legs. They didn't say much, but they didn't have to. I knew. I wasn't invited out as much anymore, and very rarely were they coming to my room to chat or hang out. I was in a house with a few hundred women, and I never felt more lonely. After the whispers came the confrontations: "Lee, are you okay?" they would inquire. "Lee, we are worried about you."

It infuriated me. What the hell did they know? Did they know what I was going through? Who were they, those friends I drank beer with and talked about boys with? They didn't know me. I never told them. The ones who confronted me were scratched off. Erased. *Not true friends. Just jealous,* I would assure myself. But then others began to confront. One night in the bar that Ryan and I frequented, I was standing next to the shuffleboard table, waiting for my turn, when Ryan's fraternity brother came to stand next to me.

"Hey, Lee," he said, this big handsome guy with dirty blond curls. He didn't miss a beat, and he confronted me too, telling me he was worried. I was "disappearing," he said. The guys in the fraternity were worried about me. Was I okay? My friend Jen also, her words a bit harsher, "Watching you do this to yourself is like watching you stick a knife in your arm over and over. You have to get help."

I was pissed at all of them, but it hit me: Something was happening to me. Something was wrong.

"I think I might have an eating disorder," I said while sitting on the couch with my Dad and Debbie, his girlfriend. My Dad had his red face on, and Debbie sat concerned, her eyes so sweet and gentle. He had tears. I saw them. Small trickles but I saw them.

"Well, let's get you some help, then," Dad said.

My hands stuffed between my thin legs. My head down. My body hot with shame. What was wrong with me that I couldn't eat? Dad scheduled an appointment with a therapist, and I began to see a dietitian at the college health clinic. The dietitian was a petite woman named Anne. She taught me what portions were and what food would look like on a plate. She had me write food diaries. I tried to comply with what she was asking because I really liked her.

The therapist, however, needed a therapist. It was easy to ask her questions and get her to talk about herself. She liked talking about herself. We would sit in her office as she flipped her long, blond hair, telling me about her ski trips, her life. I told her a few things, but mostly I just got her to talk.

I didn't want to talk. I didn't want to tell this woman anything. She was so self-absorbed, her life so cool. I was petrified to tell her anything. So I didn't.

Ryan and I still dated during this. But now I was even more mixed up. I didn't have the desire to be around people much anymore. It was a weird feeling, knowing I was now too thin yet I felt so fat, felt like I stuck out like a sore thumb. I could feel the looks, the stares at my black leggings that no longer stuck to my legs. But when I would try to eat, try to fill up my body like I was supposed to, I couldn't. The food would come at me in my mind with its numbers and calories.

I was in a tormented state of war.

I wanted people to stop staring, stop telling me how worried they were, stop walking on eggshells around me. Yet I couldn't seem to do the basic act of feeding myself.

Ryan and I took a vacation together to his hometown of Colorado Springs. I didn't tell my parents I was going, didn't figure they needed to worry anymore. That weekend we spent skiing and sitting by a fire in his parents' log cabin with his family. They were amazing. Warm and friendly, they made me feel at ease and at home. His family was so perfect, mine so chaotic. How would this ever work?

We went to a bar up near an Olympic skating rink, the smell of the rink and a fresh iciness in the bar. Fear began nibbling at me. To get too close to me meant that you could really see me. I couldn't stand the me inside. How could I let someone else see her? To be in a relationship, to really fully be in a relationship meant I had to be vulnerable and real.

I started a fight with him at the bar. His fault, I said, for some nonsense conversation we were having. Who knows what about, the argument, but I would stir it up, create the drama to make distance. To keep the control. To keep myself from getting hurt. To protect, just in case. I did it to him over and over again when I felt him getting to close, felt him loving me too much. Didn't he know I was damaged goods?

After the trip, during the time I was supposed to be getting better by seeing my therapist, we broke up and got back together many times. I no longer knew what I wanted. We finally ended it at the end of the school year. We were too close, and I was too afraid.

He sat on the floor of my room; I sat on the bed. His eyes, wet with tears. Me, now cold and hard. I told him it was over. I told him I needed to figure myself out, to find God again, to pull myself back together. It sounded nice.

Really what I wanted was to be alone in my pain. Alone in my eating disorder.

"I don't know if I can live without you," he whispered.

Stunned. Shot back like a cannon. This boy could get anyone in the world; what made him say something like that? It shocked me. I felt like someone took a boot to my heart. I knew I did, in fact, love him. I didn't love me. I hated me. How could I tell him that, how could I put that in words? He left in tears. I sat there for hours, wondering why on earth the best thing that had happened to me, I just let walk out my door. *You deserve this,* the voice said.

minnesota

My stomach grumbling for food, my mind telling it to quiet down, I slid into the driver's seat of my white Toyota and began the pilgrimage north. I was fleeing to Minnesota where I had no real connections. In fact, I had never even been to Minnesota. But I thought, *Maybe it will free me from the chains of life weighing me down.*

"You are running away. That is all you are doing," Mom said the night before when I had told her. "Running away from your family, from your life."

Whether the conversation was about the weather or my choices in life, we were like two hot irons burning the skin off each other. This conversation ended in another explosion. I sat on the floor with my knees to my chest, veins filled with heat and tears soaking my face. The pain between us was so out of control, neither one of us able to speak out loud what exactly churned beneath.

It had been a year since I broke up with Ryan, and now finishing my senior year, I had cut most relationships out of my life, even standing before the Panhellenic Council and begging to be let out of the sorority house. By then, everyone knew something was wrong with me, but instead of asking for help, I was angry and hurt by their lack of understanding. So I begged to move out. They let me. And finally, I was alone with my obsession.

The year was a blur of nothing but me constantly studying, exercising and holing up in the laundry room of my apartment, memorizing lines. I had a role as an old woman in a play called *Tartuffe*. It required a great deal of mental and physical stamina, and took up most of my time.

By the end of senior year I was so itchy in my own skin that I knew something had to change. Unfortunately, due to transferring schools, I had one more semester of credits to finish. Any change could only be for the summer. So I applied to Young Life summer staff. The application asked me to pick three places to volunteer. I chose Minnesota first, with my theater teacher's voice echoing in my mind, "To succeed in acting and to get jobs, you need to go to the work. The work is in LA, New York, Chicago and Minneapolis. Minneapolis is the home of the Guthrie Theater."

Theater was where I felt most at home. With my family consistently telling me to "be quiet" and to "stop being over-dramatic," the stage was a place where no one was shushing me.

The world I was living in felt so out of control, whereas on the stage, I knew my next line, knew the outcome and knew how long it would all take. There was a sureness in the action to come and the words to be spoken. I also found myself fueled by the audience. They were the barometer of my performance and, eventually, of whether or not I mattered. Did they laugh at the right time, shed a tear when demanded or gasp at the unexpected? It was off the stage where I was forced to face my real emotions. Once I stepped off, washed away my makeup and took off my costume, I was just me again. Back in my own skin. Back in my own realness. Not good enough.

Minnesota was going to be my place. A place where I could launch my acting career and get back into Young Life without my family shaming my religious choices. I was excited for the road ahead. My plan, once I received the acceptance letter for a Young Life camp in Minnesota where I would volunteer for a month, was to drive up for a weekend, and look for a job and a place to live.

The drive was straight and easy until tornado sirens began to bellow from somewhere across the Iowa fields. Rain pounded my car and I gripped the steering wheel tightly, leaning forward and trying desperately to stay on the road.

You are running. You are just running away. It can't be good to run away, I heard Mom saying in my head as my fingers stuck to the rubbery wheel. I clenched my teeth and narrowed my eyes. *Just drive, Lee. Just drive.* I drove fast and hard, leaving the storm behind me. As I drove up a hill, I was struck by the expansive view of Minneapolis skyline: hope and a new me. I smiled and danced in my seat.

The next morning I went to find that job. With years of waitressing experience, I felt confident I could find something. Within one hour of searching I landed a job at Pizzeria Uno, which was next to the Young Life office in a city called Edina. Josie, a friend from college, had told me a guy named Brad Pearce was the area director, that I should go meet him and maybe he could help me find a place to live.

His office was a small, narrow space with an oversized fish tank filling half the room. Brad, tall and thin, could have been mistaken for a high school kid. He was full of energy, and something about him made me feel like I had known him all of my life.

Although he wasn't the one who made the strongest impression on me.

"Hey, Chris," Brad hollered after hearing someone moving around in the lobby. "Come in here and meet my friend."

Tall and strong, Chris wore a bluish-green nylon jacket, jeans and untied running shoes. His hair, dark, held slight waves.

Brad said, "Lee is here for the summer and looking for a place to live. Do you know of anyone who might exchange housing for childcare or housecleaning?"

Chris smiled wide and said, "You can come live with us!" They both laughed. By *us* he meant his two buddies, Matt and Pete, who lived in a lake house south of where we were. I laughed back at the joke, "Ha, thanks."

"Chris also works part time at Nordic Track in Mall of America, so if you ever need anything, give him a call," explained Brad.

I filed it away in my head for later. I was on a mission, and that mission did not include another botched relationship with a boy.

I had a slip of paper with the name Brooks on it. Josie had urged me to call her, a friend she knew from Young Life. Josie was sure Brooks and I would hit it off. I called and an energetic voice answered on the other end. Brooks was leaving soon for her own Young Life assignment, but told me to call her sister Ashley. "Hey," she said excitedly, "Ashley is on summer staff at Castaway too!"

I called Ashley, who I immediately connected with. We had a great deal in common and realized quickly we would be on the same team at Castaway. I didn't know it then, but God was providing me with an army.

I returned to Kansas to finish up the semester, and by May I was back in Minnesota. This time, I made another phone call, a call to Nordic Track: "Hi, I am looking for a guy named Chris?"

"Oh, sorry," the salesperson said. "He isn't here, but you can call him at home." He gave me his home phone number without hesitation.

I crossed my legs and doodled on the paper next to me. When an answering machine clicked on, I left a message, "Hi, my name is Lee Wolfe. Not sure if you remember me, but I met you in the Young Life office. I need friends and was wondering if you would show me around?" I left the number where I was staying and hung up. I knew I had begun deep isolation in the past year, and I needed someone to help me meet people. The rigidity of my own obsession was choking the life out of me.

Judy took a message when Chris returned my call. She was the mom of one of my Young Life friends, Jeff. The mother of three boys, she embraced me as one of her own. I had a hard time relaxing into the outpouring of love this woman gifted me. Her smile so warm, her home so welcoming. *Don't love me*, I wanted to tell her. *I will disappoint you and can't give you much.* When she first showed me to my room she said, "I tried to make it more girl friendly!" The bed was covered in a soft bedspread and a vase of fresh daisies was on the dresser. I was deeply touched by her preparation for me, a mere stranger.

That first night in that house I slept messy. For the past year my sleeping posture was stiff and straight. I had to have the covers just right and usually slept in a way that barely messed the bed up. It was as if I didn't want anyone to think I actually slept. Because it would be weak to enjoy sleeping, to rest. This was another way the voice told me to deny my body.

After I finally called Chris back, we arranged for him to pick me up to hang out and listen to a band with a group of his friends.

"Sure!" I would love to, I had said, trying not to act too eager. *Hang* didn't imply date. *Hang* implied a group getting together to socialize. *Hang* was what I was looking for.

"Great! I will pick you up at seven," he said casually.

"Okay, I should probably give you the address," I said.

"Aww, nope, I know the Carvers. I know where they live." I was taken aback, having no idea he knew where I was living, but eventually I realized the tightness of the community I was being ushered into.

We rode in his green Acura, and I looked over at him—his profile so chiseled, the angles sharp and the eyes set in the middle so perfectly. This was just friends, I reminded myself. He turned and looked right through me. Embarrassed, I looked away and looked down at my thighs. *They are touching. I wish they weren't touching. So fat, these thighs. Does he see them? Squished together like pieces of lard.* I tightened them to make them look firm, just in case he looked. Even though this was platonic, I still didn't want him seeing my fat thighs.

We talked nonstop on the ride there, and I discovered a piece of important information. He had a girlfriend. I was relieved.

Inside the smoke-filled bar, the band had already begun. I was a bit nervous about how he would introduce me. My mind played options: *This is my friend. This girl needs friends. This girl is so desperate I felt sorry for her.* Or other options like, *This girl is a bit odd so please make conversation with her so I don't have to.*

I reminded myself that it was fine if they didn't like me. I could always put my things back in my brown duffle bag, jump in my Toyota and head on back to Kansas.

"This is Lee," Chris said. "She just moved here from Kansas."

They all smiled and the introductions began. Their responses were warm and welcoming. Over the noise of the band, I met the group—their smiles genuine and eyes bright. *So nice,* I thought, *this group is so nice.* His girlfriend was not there.

We chatted about the usual—where we were all from and how they all knew each other. Mostly Chris and one of the girls, Deb, did the talking. I nodded and smiled at the right times and asked questions so as to not draw the attention to myself too much. I sat relaxed, my shoulders down and my legs not wiggly like they usually were. A fresh start. The music went from acoustic to a full band, and group conversation was no longer possible. We all faced our stools forward toward the band, trying to soak in the music.

Chris had other plans.

He scooted his stool right next to mine. The smoke in the bar was heavy, but when his body was so close to me, I could feel the heat of him, the smell of cologne so rich and musky— all my senses wanted to get closer to him, that smell, those eyes. He began to ask questions, almost like he had written them down beforehand.

"So what books are you reading right now?" his eyes zoned in on me.

"Well, I am reading *Mere Christianity* by C. S. Lewis." Of course, I didn't tell him I was also reading the *Twelve Steps for Christians,* revealing way too much and possibly scaring him off. "What about you?"

"Henri Nouwen, C. S. Lewis."

I looked hard back at him, not afraid of the challenge— whatever that was.

"What do you do in your free time?" he continued.

"I like to run, read and hang out with people," I replied, even though running had been the only thing I had been doing.

"What are you hoping for your future?"

I stopped answering and looked at him, studying him, his face intent on collecting the data. "Why are you asking me all of these questions?"

He leaned back a bit. "Oh, sorry. I was just curious. Just trying to get to know you."

He laughed. I laughed. An awkward laugh meant to fill an awkward moment. We both turned our faces to the band.

Then I asked, "What do you like to do with your free time?"

It was a peculiar thing, this first night together. It was like he was sniffing me out for a reason I couldn't grasp.

II

castaway

June finally came, and I went to Castaway to volunteer for a month. Chris wasn't there, but he popped in my head at the most unsuspecting times. *A distraction*, I thought, *nothing but a distraction from my summer of retreat and introspection.* Yet he was a distraction like a force of wind, pulling me in.

Castaway was set so beautifully on a peninsula, a place for high school kids to come away from the craziness of life to experience high adventure and the gospel. It was a camp like this where I had my first encounter with God, which led me to enter a relationship with God.

I spent the month doing two things: running the zipline on a high wooden tower and raking the beach in a large tractor. I would stand for hours in the sun, teaching high schoolers the art of harnessing themselves in for safety on the zipline as it swept them into the lake. My days were spent outside, and any free time hanging with the waterfront crew, my teammates for the month. Pete, who I met on that night with Chris, was a great boss and set a standard of excellence for all of us to follow. During the day he was a respected leader, while at night we would all sit in the basement of the main building, the Windjammer, laughing until nearly wetting our pants. I felt close to God. But the dark thoughts, the self-punishment and the fears were all there too. How, in a place so serene and filled with such supportive, amazing, God-loving people, could I still feel lonely, afraid and scared?

I did.

Sometimes on the tower, when no kids were pounding up the stairs to experience the zipline, I would gaze out over the water with manic-like thoughts. The praying would start, and then the eating disorder thoughts would sneak in. *My fingers are getting fat. My cheeks are fat.* I would think about what was served for lunch, thoughts about how many calories I had consumed. As much time as I spent in my Bible, the gross, slimy thoughts of unworthiness and punishment would sneak in and cloud my head.

Why—when everything was going so well, with great friendships, wonderful time spent in nature serving God, and surrounded by supportive and amazing people—would I continue to need the eating disorder?

I was trapped by it. It was like a large oak tree, with its roots wrapped tightly around places in my mind. The harder I would try to cut free, the tighter the roots would grab me, stealing my breath. Stealing my hope.

I tried to pretend the thoughts weren't there anymore. Plus, in a Christian community, how could I share I was afraid of food, afraid of feeling? Wouldn't they tell me to let go and let God? Yes. Wouldn't they tell me to pray and God would take it? Yes. Wouldn't they tell me to have more faith? Yes. All of these things were told to me, and none of them had worked. In fact, they made me feel like a failure in the God category.

Like a tick, the eating disorder hung on so tightly it began to wear me down with its hold on me. The thoughts, like its nasty little legs, burrowed deep inside of me. *Not good enough. Devil's child. Try harder. Too much. Bad apple. Must be better. Must try harder.* All of it, a low hum, running in my mind twenty-four hours a day.

After our month-long assignment Pete invited the waterfront crew to his home back in Lakeville for a party. At an A-frame home on the lake, Ashley and I walked through the screen door into the crowd of people, many faces from camp sitting or standing in the living room. Out of the corner of my eye, I was drawn to another familiar face. One not from camp.

He strutted down the stairs at the far end of the room. A blue T-shirt and khaki shorts. Baseball hat backward on his head. It was Chris. My stomach was tickling and fluttering. At some point, Ashley got up and, before I knew it, he was sitting next to me and I was sweating. "Hey, how are you? How was Castaway?" he asked.

"It was really amazing and so much fun."

Those eyes.

Just friends, Lee. Just friends, I reminded myself.

■　■　■

Ice cream. Hot summer days, where mosquitos nibble all over any exposed flesh, the entire state of Minnesota appeared to be outside on days like this—because who knew when the temperature would dip to below zero again? We sat on the curb, the two of us, knees close. Almost touching close. Chocolate milk-shake for Chris and a vanilla cone for me. Desserts were not something I allowed myself often, but I did then. For this.

He turned to me, "Do you mind if I pray?"

"For the ice cream?"

"Yeah. Is that weird?"

We held hands and he thanked God for our time together and for the sweet treat of ice cream. I closed my eyes and felt the warmth of his large hand holding mine. So nice. I didn't know I'd been craving touch. But the warm skin of his hand enveloped mine and made me feel safe.

Then I thought of the ice cream. Why on earth would I pray for something full of fat? Something I would run off the next morning?

He finished, his voice soft, "Amen."

We walked casually around the lake. Sailboats bobbled in the water, and the night sky began to color pink. And then he told me: he had broken up with his girlfriend. I didn't ask why.

The fear deep below. What was it? I could hurt him, like I did Ryan. Like I had others. Here he was, so kind and good looking. I couldn't help but look at him, and every sense in my body was alive. I would get too close and ruin it. I didn't trust myself to successfully have a relationship. The voice reminded me of this. *Watch out. Don't get too close.*

I knew summer would end. I would return to Kansas. So I soothed the fear and the gnawing that told me to be wary with a reminder that this was short term. I waitressed at Pizzeria Uno's during the day and spent evenings with Chris. Movies, walks, late nights laughing. We spent a lot of time with his roommates, Pete and Matt, sitting around a bonfire, staring into the orange flames and talking.

Much of our time was fun and adventurous. After a movie, we'd walk through the deserted Mall of America, performing cartwheel races until we fell, dizzy, laughing at our childishness. Sometimes we sat in the car listening to Crash Test Dummies or belting out cheesy Celine Dion songs. Singing and drumming on the dashboard, we laughed together at our fun. Another evening adventure for us was pool hopping. We scouted out apartment complexes with pools, scaled the fences, and jumped in the pool or hot tub with our clothes on. Both of us, we quickly realized, loved adventure and spontaneous activity.

It became a relationship but not a boyfriend-girlfriend relationship.

I began to wonder. Wonder if he saw my pain. Saw the fear somewhere deep in my eyes. Or was it the physical me? My body, in reality, too thin. Was he not physically attracted to me? I was to him. But was he to me? And it fueled my fire: *Work out more. Eat better. Control and force the body to mold into how it should be. Not how it is. Always strive to make it better.* When I was with Chris, the thoughts were like tiny voices deep in the back of my mind. It was as if I was stronger than the voices when I was with him. I could ignore them. I could do what I wanted, eat what I wanted and even relax. But at night, alone in bed at the Carver's house, was when they would flood me. *Don't get too close. You will ruin this. How will you reach your goals if you get all mushy with a guy? Plus, don't count on this, Lee. He just wants a friend for the summer. He will forget about you when you go home.*

Mornings were spent running, running from the thoughts. Through the neighborhood of large homes towering over me, I ran the sidewalks, I ran the streets, I ran over and over again to keep myself in line.

Eventually I shared with him, "I am struggling with an eating disorder." The only guy I had ever shared this with.

I expected him to run from me. Maybe I hoped he would be disgusted by it. To even disappear.

He didn't. He asked questions.

"What do you mean? You are beautiful!"

Red cheeks. Embarrassed. *Why did I tell him this?* I wasn't looking for praise, only for him to have a deeper understanding of me. And wouldn't he run?

He didn't. He listened. He asked questions. He was compassionate. He said my eating struggles made him sad, "I am sad, Lee, that someone as wonderful and amazing as you has had these hard situations, and I am sad that you think controlling your food will help."

Opening that place in my life and letting him in was a monumental risk, as well as a bit of a test. I wanted him to see the bruised-apple side of me, the yucky parts I hated. I wanted to see if he would be able to deal. If not, I left him the option of running before we got too entangled.

Our conversation did the opposite. It brought us closer together. He shared stories of his own pain. Of things he struggled with in his head. And we connected.

Is this how God sees me too? I wondered.

leaving

Slow and steady, we walked one by one. The week before I would return to Kansas, I agreed to lead a group of ten high school students on a Young Life adventure called "Wilderness." Now the steep mountain ahead. Evergreen trees, full of the whispers of those who had walked the trail before us. The sky, a canvas of baby blue. Our hiking boots, twelve sets crunching the small branches as we made our way. I walked behind Chris, my large pack heavy on my spine. Examining, as I went, not the ground beneath me but his body so close. We trudged straight up as the weather switched seasons every few hours.

A few weeks earlier Brad had called, asking if I would be a leader on this trip. I had one more week left before returning to Kansas to finish my last few classes. Despite being a senior the year before, I couldn't receive my degree unless I finished a few dangling credits. "Of course I will go!" I said to Brad.

Surprisingly, Chris was assigned to be my coleader.

I was distracted by Chris on this journey, but I was also distracted by the *other* him: the eating disorder. Before meals, "Ed," as I had been calling him this last year, made deals with me about what I should or shouldn't eat. I overcame his demands by reminding myself of the need for fuel while climbing a mountain. *Suck it up,* I told myself.

And so I did. I ate the M&Ms. I ate the red meat. I ate whatever was served as long as I thought of it as fuel to get me up the mountain.

On our last night on the mountain, the students started asking to sleep outside under the stars. Before we knew it, all ten of them left the tent. Chris and I were alone. As leaders on a Young Life trip, the last thing we were supposed to be doing was flirting. The focus was meant to be the kids, not falling in love.

I was bundled in my bag, wool hat warming my head. Chris next to me, wearing a funny blue cap with long sides to cover his ears. Alone, the two of us.

We chitchatted about the day, and then he opened the door to the conversation that had been looming in my head the entire trip. *Are the feelings boiling inside of me my own or are they his too?*

He asked quietly, "Did it bother you to hear me talk about my old girlfriends when I gave my life story?"

I responded sarcastically for purpose, "But we are just friends."

Silence.

"Chris, let's just lay it all on the table. I am going back to KU in two days," I said.

"Long distance relationships are hard. They rarely work," he continued. Then he whispered, "Would it be okay if I kissed you right now?"

With the heat of his body next to me now, his face prickly from a week of not shaving, his lips tenderly touched mine.

We stopped abruptly. The desire awake and hot between us.

He moved away, the touch of his face still alive on my skin. Our breath heavy in the space between us. Neither of us said anything. Chris moved to the side and finally broke the silence, "Lee, let's pray for us."

Really, all I wanted to do was keep kissing. *Who could want to pray right now?*

We both prayed aloud for God's guidance in this relationship, for God to be first in our individual lives. No decisions were made about what was next, but there was an understanding, without the exchange of more words. I lay awake all night reflecting on the past three months.

So much had happened. A new state. New friends. A month of heaven at Castaway. And love. Deep, rich love like I had never experienced before.

How could it go wrong?

I felt free and hopeful and untrapped. And I had actually gained weight.

■   ■   ■

I was staring at another ceiling, this time in the living room of my apartment back in Kansas. Dad and I had scoped it out before my Minnesota summer. It was an oversized attic apartment on the third floor of an old house with no air and families of cockroaches. My white brass daybed, the only thing I still owned from my home, was nestled in the corner of my tiny room.

I wasn't ready to lie in that bed; it might mean I had come home, returning to everything I had left behind. Sliding back into the old life, I slept on an air mattress on the nasty wood floor, my brown duffle bag unpacked beside it. For a few days, I just laid there, in and out of sleep and dreams. I was sweaty and hot in my sleeping bag from the trip, but I didn't care. I wanted the smell of the damp mountain air—and the smell of him. I lived in this place of dreams. When asleep, I would see him. When awake, I would scribble like mad in my journal. Page after page with words of fear and unrest about the future ahead. The days moved on without me, and I finally got up from the floor. I went to class. I came home. I barely ate. Food meant I had to feel. And I prayed—a lot.

At the top of the hill on the campus at KU sat the tiniest chapel—a quaint spot with reddish brown wood inside, the smell was old and musty. It became my hiding place. My respite. I walked up the massive hill from my apartment, my entire body pouring with sweat from the heat, and found my spot in the front row. A cross, an altar and stained glass. I sat. I knelt. My voice echoed lonely cries. Me talking aloud to God.

Sometimes I even lay on the old, carpeted stairs and stared up into the wooden rafters. I talked to God. I cried to God. The underlying drone, so present in my life, had begun to show its head again. It was the same buzzing I had my first year of college.

In Minnesota, with all of the excitement of a new city and the passion of a new love, the hum was quieted a bit. But here, right back in the place I left, it screamed at me. I prayed and journaled and wept for relief from the noise in my mind.

I didn't find relief. I wondered if God heard me? So I talked louder. I wondered if he was too busy? I took matters into my own hands to dull the noise with frantic busyness. And then, when I was in that chapel on my knees, with the to-do list gone, the voice came back, gnawing at me. It was like an annoying, pokey finger constantly tapping me on the shoulder: *See Lee, here you are now. No friends. Nothing. What are you going to do now, Lee?*

By October the weight began falling off of me like old skin. I didn't notice at all, just noticed the voice was quieter.

Chris was my bright spot during this time. Hours on the phone. I sat against the wall, my hand twirling the cord while we talked. I shared with him about my busy life of school and activity. In reality, it was just busyness keeping me occupied. My heart ached when we hung up the phone.

We were open about our feelings for each other, and we shared missing each other with the silly love game, "You hang up first."

He laughed, "No, you hang up first."

"No, you hang up first."

Click. I missed him.

He invited me to a friend's wedding. I didn't hesitate a bit but hopped in my white Toyota and sped up there as fast as possible.

Judy and Dave said I could stay with them while in town. "Of course!" Judy said on the phone. "We would love to see you!"

As I walked through the door and into the kitchen, Judy greeted me with a big, warm hug. Chris was there too. While Judy embraced me in her arms, and planted a kiss on my forehead, he sat and waited for his turn.

My body was a sweaty mess in a knot of anxiety. *What if things are different? What if the feelings are gone? What if he has met someone else? What if, what if?* Until he hugged me. The warm smell of him stopped the worry instantly.

For some reason, I knew in that moment that I had to either give my eating disorder up or give him up. I couldn't fully engage in this relationship while also numbing myself. The problem was, now I wasn't sure I could stop.

On Saturday we had breakfast together at the Carver's house. Out on the three-season porch, the sun was just making its appearance when Chris talked sternly to me, "I am concerned about your eating."

"Why?" I said, baffled.

"You look like you lost weight. And it worries me. You didn't have any weight to lose."

I was shocked. Really, I hadn't noticed at all. Hadn't even thought about it. Except when he said something, I knew he was right.

Gotta get this fixed, I thought. And then no more was spoken of it.

We attended the fall wedding in Minnesota with lots of pumpkins, cool air and a field spread out in front of us. There were white tents for a reception and white chairs with ivory bows tied in the back. Friends, old classmates and Chris's family were also at this wedding. I met them—the hand shaking, the eye connecting, the chitchatting—all the time smiling and laughing. The night sky shone on us and we found ourselves wrapped into each other on the dance floor. He twirled and lead me through song after song. We laughed and we held tight. We kissed and we danced slow, we laughed and did the hand jive. The night was long but felt brief. My bones were tired from the dancing, the standing, the day of constant going. But my heart— that was the happiest. My heart was full. Full to the brim.

I returned on Sunday to the cockroaches and my white brass daybed. I stirred and pondered and lost sleep. I wanted to return to Minnesota. I wanted to return to the place where I felt free and alive. I asked the brown ceiling beams in the chapel, I questioned the worn carpet at the altar, I looked into the stained glass windows. I prayed for direction. The walls in that little chapel telling me to *go.*

By January I was living with a family in Minnetonka, Minnesota as their nanny.

13

the dream

The darkness at 5:00 a.m. was vastly empty. A slight glimmer from the moon and the occasional glow from a car, but the rest was black and dark down the gravel road. My feet scratched through the rocks. Five in the morning in the middle of a Minnesota winter. I couldn't live without it, even if it meant running in the cold. The bone-chilling cold meant a numb body that never seemed to warm.

Minnesota winter. Something I overlooked in my love-induced rush to move there. Long, never-ending winters with towers of snow, a gray sky and the bitter cold.

I found a job twenty minutes from the city with a nice little apartment for me in the basement. In return for lodging, I helped the two young girls to their school bus each morning while the mom worked. With only my living quarters being covered, I also waitressed at the Old Spaghetti Factory in downtown Minneapolis. My college credits transferred so I could finish my final classes at the University of Minnesota, and at the end of the semester I would still receive my degree from KU. I had quite a full schedule.

Dad was less than excited about the idea of my moving back,

due to my dangling classes still not complete. "If you don't finish college, you will owe me thousands of dollars!" he would remind me every time I spoke with him. The rest of my family was also not jumping for joy at my choice to move.

They had reason to be afraid. I had no idea.

I ran hard to escape the cold. My mind spun with lists, thoughts, plans and schedules. There was a pressing on me now. I had to make this work. I had to prove to everyone I could do this. I needed to do this. But doing things for others can lead to lost motivation quite quickly. Was the move for me? Or was the move to prove something to them, because I knew they didn't like it? Was it my desire to prove something that drove me into the ground? I don't know, but I was so deep in all of it then I wasn't questioning; I was doing. My body hadn't been nourished for the past year, and I had stopped seeing a therapist or a dietitian. My mind felt constantly frantic and couldn't compose much reflection anymore.

I couldn't outrun the fear that followed me. Living in Minnesota before was fun and adventurous. But the new move was much harder. I was in charge of making a life, an entirely different experience. My eating disorder began to take advantage when I was weak and tired, which was all the time. And the busyness I buried myself in gave me an easy excuse not to eat. I feared Chris thought I moved to Minnesota for him. Which I did. But I didn't want him to think so. I played games. I kept busy and gave him little time. I wanted to make sure he really wanted me, to make sure I was more than just a summer romance. He did want me and wanted our relationship to work.

My role in the play *Tartuffe* extended into the winter. The cast from KU was up for an award, and I had to travel to Omaha to perform. The role required I wear a heavy, ornate costume and an extremely hot, cumbersome wig. On stage I found myself dizzy and lightheaded. It was harder to remember my lines. It was harder to stand for long periods of time. I knew I was slipping again. Mom came to watch the performance. She knew too. She didn't say anything—our relationship so strained now—but she had the same look in her eyes as the girls in the sorority.

■　　■　　■

One evening we were at the new apartment Chris shared with two other guys. A huge wood bookshelf with a TV and stereo was flanked by two monstrous speakers on each side of the bookshelf. A dart board on the wall was next to a picture of a canoe. The red candle Chris had lit was the only soft addition to the place. We were on the futon, my head in his lap, my legs curled underneath me, attempting to watch a movie. I wore my thick wool sweater to keep my body warm. The movie ended with me in a deep sleep. Chris gently shook me awake, and my eyes stung when they opened.

"Lee, wake up."

I sat up, rubbing my eyes and slowly came awake. My mind reminded me of the work still left to do on my directing project for a theater class. Work still awaiting my time that night.

"Sorry, I fell asleep."

"It's okay. I know you are tired," he rubbed my shoulders slowly and gently. "Lee, I need to talk to you about something."

I was awake now. The words jolted my system to wake up. *Was he going to break up with me? Did I make a mistake in moving here?*

"Okay," my stomach twisted and my head ran in all sorts of directions of worry.

"I had this dream last night, this dream I need to talk to you about. I really feel like I need to share it with you."

I relaxed my shoulders. He took his hands off me and held them in his lap. Then he gently pulled my hand into his. I looked at him, his eyes thinking and his dark eyebrows squeezed together. He looked serious.

"It was so strange. I woke up in the middle of the night, and I remembered my dream. It was so vivid, Lee. It was like God was talking to me. I didn't want to forget it so I took a pen and paper from next to my bed and wrote it down."

I thought of stories to go with his dream. Maybe he dreamed I was hurt. He dreamed we ran off to Colorado. Or he dreamed someone died. Or he dreamed he died. Maybe he dies. Maybe he is dying. No maybe it is me; maybe I am dying.

I placed my hand on his leg, and he stopped talking. He looked down, worried, and said, "Your hand. It is so cold."

I pulled it away and forced it back into my sleeve. "Finish the dream. What happened?"

"I woke up, and I had forgotten about the dream. But later in the day I was in my room, and I noticed the sheet of paper and it came back to me. I picked up the sheet and I had scribbled Luke 2:5 on it."

I shook my head. Should I have known Luke 2:5 like everyone knows John 3:16 or something? I had no idea what Luke 2:5 meant. I was relieved when he stood up to get his Bible.

He returned to the futon with his large, black Bible open. He slowly started to read, his voice deep and low. "He went there to register with Mary, who was pledged to be married to him and was expecting a child." He paused, looked up at me and said, "Luke 2:5."

We both didn't say anything until I laughed, "Are we expecting a child? We haven't even had sex!"

He let out an obligatory laugh but didn't appear to think it was funny. This was serious, his face told me.

I waited. He said, "Lee, I think it means God wants us to get married. I have been praying for so long about it, feeling like you and I are meant to be together, feeling like I want to be with you and only you for the rest of my life. This is an answer to prayer, God telling me he ordains this!"

He leaned over and kissed me. I imagined other girls hearing the word *marriage* and seeing a wedding and a white dress and lots of flowers. I saw blankness. Nothing. Then I realized there was something wrong with me—something that needed fixing before I could see the dress, the flowers, the life with another person.

He whispered, "I love you."

"I love you too." I said the words. I felt the words. But I wanted to bolt. I wanted to leave and run and be alone. I squeezed my shoulders and clenched my jaw. I needed to be alone. I needed to be alone *now*. My body felt heavy, heavy with a burden of the words on my chest. I hated myself for feeling like this. *You idiot! Amazing, beautiful man comes in your life. Tells you he loves you. Tells you he wants to marry you. You want to run? What is your problem?* I heard the voice mocking me.

I didn't tell him my fears. I told him I needed to think about this. Needed a breath. I drove away from his apartment, hands shaking, mind racing—to Perkins to process my thoughts. I carried my large backpack into the restaurant and ordered a carafe of coffee.

I had work to do.

I had a degree to finish.

I had a scene for class to block and I needed to get it done.

But the words still tapped on my mind, over and over. And fear gripped me. My body stiff and tense and cold. I drank coffee and more coffee. I blocked the characters in the play. Moved them to stage left and stage right. I gave them movements and facial expressions. I controlled them on paper, while my own emotions seemed out of control.

Love isn't controlled. It is free and colorful and swirly with twists and turns and curls and bumps and highs and lows. Love is free. I was not free. I felt chained. Held down by something that needed unlocking first. I knew this deep down.

I loved Chris. The Lee underneath the shield of control and the layer of rigidity wanted the hair-blowing-in-the-wind, laughing love in front of me. But something preoccupied and haunted me. I felt it in my clamped jaw and tight shoulders. I knew it in my eyes that wouldn't shut and the endless amounts of coffee I poured down my throat.

At Perkins, the thoughts thrashed through me. After many hours, I finally realized what the distress was and I wrote it in my journal: *Before I can be good to anyone else. I need to learn to be able to take care of myself. Before I can become one with another, I need to let go of this baggage that follows me around. This anger so deep it grips me in the middle of the night. I need to learn to love me first. I need to really feel the love God says he has for me. But how? How do I do that? And how do I tell Chris that? Wasn't that also why I broke up with Ryan? Why I ran from him? But the cloud did come with me to Minnesota. Once the excitement of the new place set in, the same me bubbled up to the surface. And that same me needs help.*

surrender

I made a small move to face my fear. A move not to run away but to start uncovering this "stuff." A group of us were smooshed into a tiny room in a large, white church, there for a twelve-step group for Christians. Eight of us—men, women and even one teenager—we gathered together weekly to share our deep struggles. It was a goal for me to get through the twelve steps, an achievement to say I did it. So I zipped through steps one through five. I could write the answers, pour out my sorrows and appear to be changing mentally. But I wasn't changing physically.

Steps six and seven ("were entirely ready to have God remove all these defects of character," and "humbly asked him to remove our shortcomings") became my roadblock, meant I had to change. Really, step one was where I was stuck—admitting I was powerless over my eating disorder—but it took me until step six to realize it.

The day after talking about steps six and seven in our little group, a radical change took place in my life.

"Did they like what you were wearing?" Mom would inquire after the first day of school. "Did they compliment you on your new outfit?"

Really, wasn't that what becoming a little lady was?

But this little lady was disappearing quickly. Outfits were no longer pretty, ladylike things but baggy, formless garments. In the mirror, I saw something different. I saw bad things, things and places that shouldn't exist, needed perfecting, needed work. I was the worker intent to fix it.

This wasn't really a defect of character; this was my own coping skill. The two didn't go together. And my shortcomings? I already knew what those were; they were on my mind every moment of every day.

And measurement was another thing. The scale. In the morning, after a meal, before a run, after a run. Always the scale. The number was my barometer for the day.

The amount of calories consumed and the amount of energy expended. For a girl who wasn't so hot at math, the calculations came easy and constant. I looked down at the feet, the long toes, the shivering legs, and saw a number meant for a child.

I paused.

Stepped off and then stepped on again. The number the same. I had wanted a low number, but it was so low that I was a tiny bit afraid.

I walked up the stairs, to the living room in the house I was staying in. No one home. The kids I was responsible for in the mornings were at school and the mom was out shopping. I called my mom, cordless phone in hand, and nervously paced the cream carpet. I don't know why she was the first one, but isn't your mom always the one you want to call? The one who can tell you, "It is going to be okay. You are going to be all right." The one who can put a warm washcloth to your head and say, "There, there." Even if she didn't say that, I still wanted to call her first.

"Hi, Mom."

"Hi, sweetheart, what's new?"

"Not much. How about you?"

"What's wrong?" That's the thing about moms, they can always sense it in your voice—at least my mom could.

I didn't hesitate, "I got on the scale today and the number was really low. Maybe there is something wrong, my thyroid or something?"

There was a long pause on the other end, which was quite rare for Mom.

She said firmly into the phone, "Either you come home right now, or I am coming to get you."

I was shocked and confused. I had no idea why she would say something like that. But deep down I knew. I knew there was something wrong, something bigger than me sucking me away. Something I was no longer controlling but was controlling me. I knew I was powerless over "Ed" and needed help. I knew if I wanted a life worth living, I had to humbly reach out for help.

What happened next was a whirlwind. I called Chris right away and told him, but he wasn't as alarmed, said maybe I should go and get help. Within the next two days I had quit my jobs, packed everything up in my brown duffle, and was somehow willing to go.

If there were events that happened in between, I can't say what they were. I only know that I went willingly. Was I running from Chris and his dream? Maybe. Was I aware of the frailty of my health? No.

As quickly as I had come into Minnesota, my exit was just as fast.

I was a bit shocked myself that I went, because when did I ever listen to my mom's advice? This time I did. Got in a car with Brooks, who drove me almost to Des Moines, while Chris followed in his car. Des Moines was the halfway point to Kansas. They decided I was okay to make it the last three hours alone. A weathered old truck stop called the Boondock Cafe was where we said our goodbyes. They hugged me and told me to take care of myself.

I was absent from my body and in such a state of shock that the memories flash in broken pieces. I don't know how I made it alone from Des Moines back to Kansas, but somehow I did. I can't remember if Chris and I cried, if we were civil, if we broke up, or if we kissed passionately. Numb. I was completely numb.

I was surrendering. Or was I?

Woken up to the rich aroma of coffee. I was at Dad's house. The room, full of picture frames with happy smiles—smiles in Hawaii, smiles with braces, smiles from birthday parties. Our family, neatly framed, neatly hung. For a moment, it felt like any other visit to Kansas.

I knew better. My stomach told me so.

There was a distinct sense I was in trouble. The principal-calling-your-parents kind of trouble, like the time I hammered Brandy Moore's finger in wood-shop class in sixth grade. But I was an adult now, and the trouble was embarrassing. I would have done anything to crawl under the covers and pretend this day wasn't happening.

I showered and then stood in the room of smiles and gazed down at the clothes in my bag.

What does one wear for their first day as a patient in a psy-chiatric ward?

I picked out a clean pair of button-fly Levis and a yellow polo, heavily starched. As if it mattered. I weaved the brown braided belt through the loops. *When people are on trial they have them dress conservatively, so maybe if I dress like I am normal, they will see I am normal and let me go.* I sat on the bed, pulled up my white socks and tied my Keds. I made the bed exactly as it was when I arrived the night before, hospital corners and pillows placed precisely right.

Quietly I made my way down to the kitchen where Dad was drinking coffee and sitting casually at the brown table. He was reading the paper. His round face freshly cleaned. He looked up at me with his bright, blue eyes tinted with sadness, "Good morning, LeeWolfe."

"Good morning."

"Do you want some breakfast?" he asked.

"No, thanks."

I walked past him to the counter, grabbed the cup set out for me, poured a cup of coffee and placed my back against the cold counter. Dad came near me to pour himself another cup too. He leaned against the stove and stared into his mug, then his watch, then into his cup. Anywhere but into my face or my eyes.

The silence sliced my heart.

We stood there, drinking our coffee, staring out into the center of the kitchen, the two of us unable to find anything worth saying. Inside of me, there was a little girl begging, *Daddy, please don't make me go. I promise I will be better. Please don't make me; I will be good. I will try my hardest, and eat and not exercise. Please, Daddy.*

She didn't speak. Her voice gone.

"Are you ready?" he asked.

"Sure, let's go," I whispered.

The big, white hospital was near the blue house I lived in with Mom and Joe, though Mom now lived in a condo and had a new boyfriend named Charlie. Dad parked and the two of us walked through the front door. More silence and the smell of rubbing alcohol greeted us. I felt nauseous. We rode the elevators to the sixth floor. Home of the psychiatric unit. Exactly where I wanted to be at twenty-two years old.

Not the Broadway dream I had planned.

The elevator doors opened, and we saw Mom standing in the hall. Her hair falling gently on her shoulders, her outfit overly embellished with a blue bedazzled jean jacket and bangle bracelets up her arm. As I walked toward her, I was overpowered by the scent of exotic flowers. It was as if she bathed in the perfume. I used to love that smell; now I despised it. Her lips curved to the right and she bit the inside of her cheek. Her "face" was on. The same face she wore when she was pulled over for speeding. "I am innocent officer. I just have no ideaaaa how this happened," she would drawl.

Today it was the same look of innocence. "Why, Doctor, I just have no idea how she ended up like this! Our family doesn't have any problems," her face said.

"Hello, Terry," Dad said.

Twenty years of memories that birthed three lives stood between them.

I put on my good-girl smile and dug my hands deep into my pockets. The three of us walked down the sterile, narrow hallway together. Cold, crisp air with a smell of burnt coffee and too many cleaning chemicals made my skin goosebump. The nurses' station was marked with a sign, "Unit 6."

Dad talked to the woman at the desk. She gave us a look, stopped at me, then called someone on the phone. I turned to see a short, round woman walking toward us. She wore hospital scrubs with little animals stamped on them. Her hair, red and puffy. Waddling closer, I couldn't help but smell the hair spray spritzed on her frizzy nest.

I was dizzy. I wanted to run. Back to Minnesota. Far away

from here. Back to Chris. My mind screamed: *Please don't make me stay here. I don't need to be here. I don't belong here. I just lost a little too much weight. That is all. No big deal. I can just try harder and put the weight back on.*

The short, round woman had bulging eyes—the kind where there is too much white and not enough eye. She looked like a ladybug. She guided us to a hospital room and told us to have a seat.

Everything was peach. I hated peach. Bricks painted peach. Walls painted peach. No real color but peach. I sat stiff on the white hospital bed while Dad and the ladybug nurse pulled up plastic chairs. Mom stood at the end of the bed. Her shoulders back, arms crossed tightly in front of her, lips curled into a tight ball.

Mom noticed me looking at her and the lips moved into a comforting smile. Her mother eyes looked at me and told me it was going to be okay. Those same eyes had comforted me as a little girl when I had a bad dream, when I didn't get invited to a birthday party or when I just wanted a hug.

I wanted to be back there, to those times.

Ladybug held a clipboard and pen ready to strip away the last vestiges of my dignity. In rapid-fire succession, the questions came.

"What is your name? Your age? Where do you live? What year is it? Who is the president of the United States? When was your last menstrual period? Have you ever had suicidal thoughts? Are you allergic to any medications?"

I answered them as quickly as the nurse asked them, eager to end the embarrassment but horrified to be asked about my menstrual cycle and suicidal thoughts in front of my father. The blood shot up my face, and my armpits began to sweat. I wanted to hit her in the face and pop out her stupid eyes.

I answered quietly, "I don't remember when my last period was, and I don't know if I have had suicidal thoughts."

Ladybug barely skipped a beat.

"Does anyone in your immediate family have a drug or alcohol problem?" she asked.

The question swept through the room like a fog. Mom was holding her breath. Dad, the pillar of strength, answered the question for me. His eyes turned to the floor, "Yes, I am an alcoholic," he said.

Mom's face lost color. I looked into Dad's big blue eyes and saw them shine with water. Water from tears he didn't want us to see. It was all I could do to not jump up and down, and scream "Hallelujah!" Finally someone in this family was coming clean about their struggles. *Maybe Ladybug will admit him to the hospital and not me,* I wondered silently.

She didn't look up from her paper.

I wanted to stop time when he said that. I wanted Dad to hold me, to tell me it would be fine, that he would stop drinking, that he would get help too. But an entire world stood between us. An entire world with no words.

She finished her examination and told Mom and Dad they would need to leave soon. She waddled out and left us to our goodbyes.

Legs crossed, top leg kicked frantically up and down. My head full of little white stars, my stomach churning. What next? I had no plan. No goal. No schedule. I wanted to move my legs fast so I could get out of there.

Dad got up. He wrapped me into him and hugged me tight. I wanted to stay there forever, the Old Spice Daddy with donuts. *How did I get here? Please, Daddy, don't go. Please don't make me stay here.*

"I love you, LeeWolfe," he said.

Mom then came over and hugged me. I looked up at her big,

blue eyes and saw them overflowing with tears. I imagined I knew what she was thinking. *How will she tell her friends?* I wondered. *How embarrassed she must be. How unladylike this all is.*

I was not the daughter they wanted.

I hurt them. Hurting them also hurt me hard. They turned slowly and the two of them left me. Alone. In a cold, peach room in a Kansas hospital. They had no choice. I couldn't seem to take care of myself.

I curled into a fetal position on top of the white sheets and put my frigid hands between my knees. I cried. I wanted to be eleven again. Back in my flowered, pink bedroom with my dog, Pepper. I wanted to be in college again, laughing with friends. I wanted to be in my white brass daybed listening to records. Warm, thick tears streamed down my face.

I felt totally alone.

I thought about praying. I thought about asking God for help, but I was brutally embarrassed, painfully ashamed. Why would God want to listen to me after all I had done to the body *he* gave me? I couldn't talk to him. How would he understand? I had failed him. I had failed my family. I had ruined my life.

Ed was there in my head, offering me guidance: *If you just lose a couple more pounds then you might feel better. Everything will be better if you lose those last two pounds. If you lose a few more, then maybe you won't have to feel all of this. Just a couple more. Then you will be able to stop thinking about weight so much and finally move forward in life.*

mania

In my dream, I heard someone loudly call, "Lee! Lee?"

It wasn't a dream; my eyes snapped open. Above me was hovering a very large woman. She instructed, "Lee, honey, it is time to have lunch. Here, I will show you where to go."

As my body and mind woke up, I quickly remembered where I was. It made me sick inside. The woman was Peggy, another nurse, quite overweight in her shape but gentle and motherly. Her eyes were inviting and comforting. Ed joked with me, *At least she has her eyes going for her.* And then he reminded me, *But she is probably jealous of your willpower.* Ed scolded, *If you aren't careful here, you will leave this place looking just like her.*

Ed was mean and brutal, no longer a friend; he was now a warden in my prison of his making. He was demanding and would say anything to keep me trapped. I no longer had a voice to fight back, with Ed's voice so much louder.

Down the bright hall, illuminated with dreadful fluorescent lights, we walked into the cafeteria. She told me to go to the big silver cart and look for the tray with my name on top of it. I did what she said and carried my tray to a nearby table and sat down.

I lifted the purple plastic bubble covering my plate and almost passed out at the mere sight and smell of whatever had been plopped onto it. *No way in hell am I going to touch that food.*

I looked around at the others, about twelve zombielike people. Very few were talking, and a hum of conversation could barely be heard. Most ate and stared at the food. I couldn't eat. No matter how hard I tried, knowing it was what would get me out of there, I couldn't.

Next to me was a woman named Sue, a tiny lady with miniature wire glasses. In a mousy voice, she told me we were roommates. Everything about Sue seemed so fragile, I was afraid to look at her in case she broke. Ironically, she later told me she thought the same of me.

Ladybug nurse came in with another big silver cart. She looked like an ice-cream vendor. One by one she called us to her stand to hand us a little white cup filled with colored pills. She called my name, and I dutifully took the first of what would become many doses of medication during the course of my stay there.

I looked down at the pill. It was peach.

I didn't know what the pill was, just that I was supposed to take it. I did. Then I returned to the table and listened to Sue talk about her life as a nurse in oncology. She missed a medication for a patient, or forgot to do something, and felt responsible for the patient's death. She began to cry. I listened and consoled. Stars spun again in my head, but I focused on her, listening, befriending.

Trays were returned to the silver cart, and not a person in the room noticed I didn't eat.

God must have brought me here, here to help others, I thought as I nodded and smiled and gave advice to other patients.

Later we were told to go to the group room, and we sat in a

circle in the hard plastic chairs. A sad, older woman about my mom's age stared at the floor, and then another really pretty girl said hi to me. I sat down next to her, and she told me her name was Angie. Stars from not eating began to fade in my head. I noticed my legs felt heavy. The group leader came in—dark eyes, dark hair, small body. He talked about rules and hospital stuff. I bounced my leg up and down, wanting to leave, to get out of there so badly. I looked at the people, the crazy people. I was not like them. I was nothing like them. *I don't belong here. I don't belong.*

The exercise equipment in the corner of the room caught my eye, and I began to plan how to use it. But then I noticed a shiny gold plaque. It read, *In Memory of Sean Hulse, 1990.*

My classmate. Killed himself. I remember thinking back then how sad it was when Sean died, and I couldn't understand why anyone would take his own life. *Had he spent time here? Did he kill himself here? Am I like him?* I told myself, *I am not crazy. I am not like him. All these people, sitting around whining about their lives, I am* not *like them.*

Shaking my leg and chewing my gum, my own skin began to irritate me, and I wanted to crawl out of it. After sixty minutes of sitting in the cold chairs, we were finally released. I found coffee and drank it down, bitter and hot. It scalded my tongue, but I didn't care. Biting taste and pain felt good, and the coffee rushed down my throat into my empty stomach. I sulked down the hall to a room with large, overstuffed couches and one giant television. I found a spot in the corner of a worn-out blue sofa. Peach pill kicked in. Heavy eyes. Noise in my head quiet now, I passed out on the old couch.

Day after day was the same in Unit 6. No change. Just peach. And bland and boring. Routine. Wake up to a nurse taking my blood pressure, pretend to eat, take little pills, go to group, take a nap, pretend to eat. I also played ping-pong and listened to other people's problems. I comforted them, wrote them encouraging notes and tried to help.

I thought of myself as president.

I was like this the whole time I lived on Unit 6. While the doctors and nurses didn't notice I wasn't eating, they were still prescribing a diet of plenty of mood-altering medications. The less I ate and the more I took those pills, the more I wanted to crawl out of my skin. A mania unlike any all-nighter at college ensued, and I couldn't get my mind to shut off.

But I found that a little bit of clever went a long way. "I really need to get some fresh air," I told one of the nurses. She complied. My compliance as a patient, in her opinion, was due a reward. She offered me a pass to leave the unit to go to the gift shop.

I didn't need the gift shop.

I needed an escape from the ruminating with the ticker tape of thoughts. I found that escape in the basement of the hospital with the long white hallway. Pipes were exposed from the ceiling, and table linens and equipment were stored there. My running track. The air was hot and thick, and I was craving sweat.

I wanted the thoughts to stop.

I felt completely and utterly out of control in my own body and this—the running, the fast heartbeat, the sweating—was the only relief. Back and forth, like a caged animal I ran that hall. The guilt, the embarrassment, the shame, the anger, the calories, the unrelenting thoughts and the eating-disorder voice stronger than ever, chanted about burning calories, burning fat: *You must run. You can't get fat. If you let out your emotions, who knows what will happen? They might lock you up forever. No, the only way to let it out, Lee, is to run. Run. Run. Listen to me. I will take care of you, keep you controlled and keep you safe.*

I tried to run off the emotions that had now been ignored for almost two years.

I ran, and Ed counted the calories burned. I ran, and I punished the body that was too difficult to exist in. My escape. My freedom. And it almost killed me. Every day I played the good girl on the unit, listened to other patients, forgot to eat and found my space on the track in the basement.

Coffee and more coffee. My hands trembled and shook, my mind raced like a wild animal, hungry for food. But there was no food and there was no sitting still for me. I frantically colored hundreds of pages of intricate designs. I talked incessantly to patients and I moved. I moved everything: my legs, my hands, my feet. My mind had raced away, and I felt I lost it.

The staff noticed, but shockingly, didn't add the equation up that I needed food and not drugs. Food. The body, my body, living on only one source of nutrition—coffee. *Why don't they see that?* I wondered. *Because eating disorders aren't understood? Or because they are so used to diagnosing other mental illnesses?*

I didn't know. But the mania led me to a place I can only imagine would be similar to a day on crack cocaine. Stars and lightness, floating where I—the person, the body—was no longer attached.

They tried to tame me by filling me with a powerful drug. Two problems resulted: (1) I was a like a rabid, caged animal. (2) I didn't have the diagnosis they were drugging me for.

And one other piece of the puzzle: drugs don't work so well on someone who hasn't eaten in days.

They eventually resorted to confining me to my room. For forty-eight hours, in a square room with peach walls, I marked time by throwing tennis balls against walls, then markers, then shoes. All of which they took away. I was revolting against their confinement.

The psychiatrist finally entered my cage. His eyes drooped, with dark bags underneath. My memory is of a man who was almost hunchback-like, with eyes sagging so low they looked cartoonish in their extreme size. But, then, I wasn't in the sanest of minds. He stood over me while I attempted to sit still on my bed in the square room. He scolded me for my behavior, for the franticness. Really, he was scolding me for not slowing down. The same scolding that had followed me my entire life: "Slow down." "Be quiet." "You are too much."

In my disorganized and scattered state, I took his scolding as an attack on my God-given personality. As much as I tried to change me—to mold myself into the world's expectations of a girl who was ladylike, who sat nicely in a chair, who talked calmly and listened intently—I was not that girl. I couldn't be that girl.

My entire life, up until this point, I had been trying to fit this girl into this mold everyone told her she *should* be. Trying to become the person they *wanted* me to be. Trying to not be the hyperactive, talkative, spazzy thing I was.

I couldn't do it anymore. I was tired. Tired of trying. Tired of failing.

But there was another part of this frantic feeling: grandiosity. I believed, somehow, that I was unlike any other human. I don't know if it was the drugs or the not eating, but I believed I was invincible. I didn't need to eat. It wasn't necessary. So I didn't.

And I felt it crucial to make sure the doctor knew he wasn't in charge of me. I was stronger than him. I would defy all expectations of what he wanted me to do there. "I bet you," I told him confidently. "I don't need food. I can go without eating. Not everyone needs food."

He laughed, "Sure. Sure, Lee." Ignoring me, he continued,

"Whatever it is that is driving your car to destruction, Lee, has got to stop. You are sad. You are afraid of not appearing 'all together.' You are afraid to be real."

I knew deep down, in the core of me, that he was right, but I didn't dare give him the satisfaction. So I stared at him. Hard. My head was light, so I focused hard to stare him down.

He continued, "Lee, you have clinical depression and a very critical case of anorexia nervosa. It is time you face what is really going on."

That was the first time I had heard those words as a diagnosis. I didn't understand, and I didn't like it. I didn't want to hear it. I just knew I wanted to crawl out of my skin. What was I supposed to do now? Where was I supposed to go from here? I couldn't make sense of it all. I couldn't put it all together. Nothing flowed. I didn't speak anymore, and he scribbled something on his paper and walked proudly out of the room.

The day or days—I am unsure—became a black nothingness. The movement in my body had been subdued, most likely due to the pills. I was thrown down, physically, spiritually and mentally. I buried myself under the covers and refused to emerge.

The floodgates were opened, and the emotional waterfall began to flow hard and fast. I knew the doctor was right. It was time to stop hiding, time to let whatever had been stuffed away flow out.

I curled up in a ball, my shoulders shaking profusely and my insides trembling everywhere. Snapshots flowed in and out of my mind: the funeral, the fighting, the crying, the anger, the conversations, the words. Everything that was locked away in that secret place called "emotions" suddenly came out. I was letting it free, the emotions and the feelings Ed tricked me into hiding. My mind turned into a spinny ride at the amusement park.

My body couldn't handle the flood from my eyes or the merry-go-round in my head. Faster, faster, faster it went. The tears, my heart, my breath, the pain. I curled my knees up to my chest and gripped my arms around them. I squeezed myself tight, hoping to make the eruption settle.

A nurse rushed to my side and placed her hand on my back, "Lee, are you okay?"

I didn't answer. I didn't open my eyes. I just released sobs surfacing from somewhere deep in my soul. She left me and returned with another pill.

"This will make you feel better," she said

Confusion. Utter confusion. Like driving the wrong way down a one-way street, being unable to find the way out while oncoming cars were racing toward me everywhere I looked. *Why,* I wondered, *am I told to "express my emotions" and then, when I do, I am told to "take a pill to make it better"?*

I barely opened my eyes to see the delicate hand in front of me holding out a little pill. Her other hand held a blue Dixie cup of water. I took both.

I felt drunk. Everything moved like a slow-motion movie. The droopy-eyed doctor came in again, and I told him, "I bet I can get my heart to stop." Because, really, I had already stopped living, stopped feeling, stopped communicating.

"Lee, we would never let you do that!"

"I'll bet you!"

I tried not to get out of bed until my bladder made it impossible not to. I gave in and wobbled to the bathroom. Before I had time to stop the merry-go-round in my head, my mind went black.

I felt the cold, hard floor hit the back of my head.

I lost the bet.

menninger

I sat slumped in the passenger seat while Mom drove in silence. On the left we passed Lawrence, my college town. Brick buildings hovered over the graduates and the families of graduates that would descend on campus in a few weeks. I wouldn't be at the graduation. I slid lower in my seat. Me, all fragile and weak and cold. Them with heads held high, receiving their diplomas. I wouldn't be there. I would be taking little pills and learning how to eat. Mom drove the car. I sat in silent shame.

We arrived in Topeka, Kansas, at a hospital called Menninger.

Dad informed me earlier on the phone that day, "They specialize in eating disorders." The doctor had a different explanation: "It is a locked unit. They can help you." *Gee, thanks,* I wanted to say. Did I want help? Did I really care anymore to be helped? The doctors on Unit 6 said I was doing this to myself, and that I was the one causing the pain, and, "Gosh, if you would just eat." Oh, and I couldn't forget the financial burden it was for my family. While Chris was aching for me to return to my life in Minnesota. Shouldn't I have wanted that?

Large, black wrought-iron gates greeted us. I pretended we

were going to visit friends in a British castle while we drove up the winding road. Imagining this helped keep me from jumping out of the moving car. The idea of a locked ward gave me images of witchlike nurses with long needles and straitjackets. The tallest building had an enormous, old clock on it. Beautiful, yet the place sent a sharp shiver up my spine. The exterior was like that of an Ivy League college campus, but inside I knew. It was a hospital for crazy people like me.

EDU, the eating disorders unit, is where I was going. A nurse on Unit 6 had said to me, "You don't have fight left in you anymore, and the eating disorder voice is too strong. When that happens, you need someone to do it for you. To fight for you until you get your voice back."

Walking through the enormous glass doors that clicked loudly behind me, I knew she was right. I surrendered to it. Sort of.

Mom and I sat across from each other at a small, round table in a little room. Her eyes soft and gentle. I was weak and tired. I saw in those eyes the parts of the mother I loved, the same mother that looked down at me and said, "Yes, Sunshine, I know." Those eyes told me she loved me, that despite our differences she would do anything for me—would do anything to see me get well again. *Then choose it,* the voice said. *Choose to get well. Why can't you just eat? Why can't you get motivated and sit at that darn table and put that food in your mouth?* I looked down at the floor, the carpet all ragged. What was wrong with me? This human need, yet I couldn't do it. I couldn't do the simplest task that one is born doing.

I crossed my legs, which never stopped shaking, and chewed hard on the gum in my mouth—constantly shaking and constantly chewing. I couldn't stop it anymore; the body ran and moved without me. It was now an unconscious habit I couldn't control. I sat like a wadded-up blanket, a person dissolving in a sweatshirt that hung on my fragile body.

I had disappeared, and neither of us knew the road back.

March 22, 1995

Initial assessment and diagnosis:

The patient is a twenty-two-year-old Caucasian, single female who has recently been living in Minnesota where she is a senior in college. She is originally from Kansas City. She was brought in for hospitalization by her parents who were concerned regarding her inability to eat, her weight loss and depression.

The patient also reported a very severe low mood. During the last two years she has had a low mood, but it had become particularly worse in the last month. Two years ago she had several losses: her mother and stepfather divorced, her aunt, grandfather, and mother's boyfriend died. Her father moved in with his girlfriend. Her sister and brother moved out of the house. She reported proximal and terminal insomnia. Prior to being put on medication during a previous hospitalization, she was sleeping only two to three hours per night. She had no enjoyment in activities. She had poor concentration and felt constantly tired. She had suicidal ideation with a plan to overdose. She had poor self-esteem. She denied any hallucinations. She did give a history of increased activity and racing thoughts. It was usual for her to arise early, have activities scheduled all day, eat very little and go to bed around 2:00 a.m. She denied any grandiose or paranoid delusions, any feeling of euphoria, or any difficulties caused by her actions during these periods.

There was no running in the basement at Menninger, no skipping meals or drinking coffee. Bathrooms were locked, and when we were allowed to go, a nurse stood outside the door to watch for symptom use. There was even a room called the "quiet room," a padded room where patients would go when the screams were too loud or the fits too disruptive. I saw this happen in the middle of the night to a young girl. A single scream. And then a siren of screams all burst from one set of lungs. She was maybe fifteen or sixteen years old. "Schizophrenic," the other patients whispered when she arrived on the unit. Screams prompted running feet and then I saw her held by one of the strong male nurses, her arms wrapped tight in a straitjacket, her body sent to the padded room. And silence returned.

The unit where we lived had a long, brown hall with patient rooms on both sides. A common area at one end had art supplies in every corner, round tables, brown couches with worn-out covers and an enormous television. There was also a sliding glass door, where the patients could escape onto the deck to smoke. Meals were watched and timed to make sure we didn't hide our food, cut it into tiny pieces, obsess about what was on the plate or take an eternity to eat it. I did all of those things. The staff member would sit at the end of the table, on alert to police our eating. There was a construction-paper sign with colorful ink on the wall that said, "If you don't eat all of the food in the allotted time, you will receive a replacement." The replacement was a high-calorie shake that tasted like liquid chalk.

After meals we were to sit. Usually we had to sit for an hour—sometimes more depending on your unit status—so we didn't run off and throw up or try and exercise the calories away. You gained status on the unit by following the rules and gaining weight. Days were clocked away with hours of sitting and hours of therapy: activity therapy, family therapy, individual psycho therapy and relapse-prevention therapy. Theoretically we were to "talk" about our feelings without using the eating disorder as a way to hide.

I felt like a prisoner. I felt like I had committed a crime.

I found a total of two things at Menninger that made me happy: a very large, old, soft recliner and my yellow Walkman cassette player.

This chair made me feel safe from the world. It was the only place where I found rest. I claimed it as mine and everyone knew not to sit in it. The material on the chair was absent of fluff or cushion, but I curled my body like a caterpillar into a ball in this chair. Compact me, snuggled tight into it like a womb. The only place I found rest. Nurses ruined my slumber every night, making me go to my room.

"Against the rules to sleep in a chair," they said.

"Why?" I fought back.

"Against the rules. You don't need to know why."

Prisoners didn't need to know why the rules existed.

But in my room there was no sleep. The bed hard and spacious with me in it, and hours on hours of me staring at the blank, white ceiling. Unprotected and scared of I don't know what, I stared.

After the night of the girl being sent to the padded room and another night where a girl tried to set herself on fire with her cigarette lighter, I no longer could sleep unless I was in my chair. So I took matters into my own hands. The nurse would enter my room and shine her too-bright flashlight into my eyes to check for life. I would wait until I heard her down the hall, entering other rooms, and then I'd tiptoe into the little room where my chair waited. I heaved it, in all its heaviness, and dragged it awkwardly into my room. There I found deep sleep, all snuggled in a ball, with my head rested on the armrest. For a few nights. Until they discovered my extravagance and took it away.

The only important thing to staff seemed to be medication and food. But my problems were still not solved by medication and food—at least I didn't think they were. *You just need to try harder, Lee. That's all. Try harder. You didn't do enough.*

But I found another simple pleasure in my Walkman. Chris sent me tapes of a singer named David Wilcox. I sat through the hours with those headphones on while I disappeared into the acoustic realness of the words to his songs. Mostly, the songs matched my numbness, like "Frozen in the Snow." I felt frozen. Frozen in life. With no aspirations and no real hopes. This numbness led me to a very dark place.

Many of the girls talked about cutting and the relief it gave them. In utter despair one day, I took a light bulb, broke it and proceeded to slice up my arm. The pain brought relief. *You deserve punishment. You deserve to hurt for all you have done to everyone.* Without my eating disorder, cutting became the only way that I could obey the voice.

Here there was no talk of God or faith. It was eating, and eating and more eating. That would make me well, they said. *God wouldn't be in a place like this*, the eating disorder would tell me. *Not with a bunch of people who were using the temples he made to destroy themselves.* It was no wonder they never talked about God. But it froze me. *Without God, what is the point?* I wondered. But I had failed God. How could I go to him now?

Mom had thought my faith was yet another "extreme" part of my personality, and I was starting to believe she was right.

■   ■   ■

The summer after Young Life camp, I wanted to share my new faith with my mom, as well as the cool things I was learning about God. So I wrote her a letter. On my blue spiral notebook,

I carefully crafted words that expressed my heart on the page. I shared with her my experience at camp, what I was learning from the Bible, and I asked for forgiveness.

I think that was the line that made her afraid. Me, asking for her forgiveness for all the times I had said mean things. Words like "I hate you." Or when I would yell, "You're the worst mom in the world." I wanted her to forgive me because I had just read that God wanted me to honor my mother and father. I wanted her to know this, that I was sorry.

She didn't like it. Not at all. To her it was akin to me saying things happened that she never believed happened. It was inability to recollect "ugly words," as she would call them, that were not necessary to talk about. So for me to spell it out on paper, in ink for her to read, that really upset her. She sat in the wingback chair in our blue house with Joe, waiting for me.

I saw her from the kitchen as I entered. I sensed not a reconciliation coming, but something different. A reprimand. A scolding. A mother now concerned for her daughter. The conversation was brief and sharp. The clearest memory I have is of seeing her concerned face, brows pinched together, jaw tightly clenched, hand gripping the paper: "You are going to the extreme. You are taking this 'Christian' thing too far," she said. "You are scaring me with all of your religious talk. You need to be careful of this group; they might be brainwashing you," she scorned.

■　　■　　■

And then, while I sat like a caged animal, I began to wonder if she was right.

back pockets

My family came and visited me like I was an animal in a zoo. That made me feel worse. Mom, Dad and Debbie (my dad's girlfriend) made the long trip over and over again to see me. I felt terribly guilty. It became like a storm that wouldn't relent: Guilty for the cost, guilty because I couldn't get better. Mom repeated to me, over and over, with tears filling her eyes, how much she loved me. Dad did the same. And I was flooded with more guilt.

What were they supposed to say? What would have helped me then? What they did say did help me. It really did. Despite my guilt and shame, their acknowledgment and me knowing their love was there in spite of what had occurred over the past few years became a lifeline somewhere deep in my soul. As I watched some of the other patients without the support, without families who were carrying the hope for them, as mine were for me, I knew their love was a life preserver I needed to hold on to. It was risky, but I knew I had to let them carry the hope for me. Because I couldn't.

My individual therapist was a little man with a thick, gray beard, like a miniature Santa Claus. I talked while he scribbled on a yellow notepad. In his office, in the tower with the large clock, I was first able to uncover the layers of hidden feelings that had been masked by the eating disorder. I realized my deep fear was not about food but about feeling. I discovered I was petrified to cry or scream. If I did, I might not ever stop. But he slowly helped me begin to pour those feelings out in his office.

The family work was done in sessions led by a woman named Joan. She had scraggly, white hair and she wore long, white dresses that looked like bags with old Birkenstocks on her feet. She was the picture of Woodstock. During one session, I whispered to Mom how unladylike I thought her attire was and Mom agreed. "Not ladylike at all," she said.

"We are talking today about why Lee doesn't feel good enough," Joan blurted out as my face turned red.

"Not good enough?" Mom said, shocked. "We gave you everything you ever needed and more. We had you in everything you wanted. We are always telling you how wonderful you are. How could you think that?"

"I just do. I just do," I said.

And I remembered. In that office, I remembered when I first knew I needed to try harder.

■　　■　　■

It was the day Dad had a family meeting in the house where the basement was being remodeled. I was twelve. We were in their large bedroom with pretty yellow-and-white wallpaper. Mom was not there. I walked in and Dad was sitting at the faded yellow desk. His head down, mouth closed and shoulders slumped. I paused before entering.

My daddy. The strong one.

I was frightened. I didn't know what to do, how to do any of this. Kristin walked in and found a spot on the bed. I followed her, and I wanted to yell into the thick air of the room, "No! No!"

But I sat on the large four-poster bed where hundreds of mornings had been spent cuddling with Mom and Dad. Corky came in and took a seat on the floor, underneath the narrow window. I needed air, and I could hear my heart thumping in my chest. I had overheard the words of Mom's telephone conversations: divorce, divorce, divorce.

Dad got up and walked slowly to the old rocking chair in the corner next to Corky. The wood creaked from a body that was heavy with life. The moments happened like a dream, like they weren't really happening as they were happening. Words came out deep and long. I heard bits and pieces.

"A new apartment."

"Come visit."

"I am so sorry."

And then I saw tears. Tears and a face red, not because of the Long Branch but because of pain, anger and hurt—adult stuff he wore on his face. He rocked back and forth, his hands gripping the chair. Back and forth. Back and forth. This is the first time in my life I had seen him cry, and it made my own body shake into a volcano of tears, fear and fright.

And I shook. And I kept quiet.

Why does he need a new apartment? I know why, but why?

Why does he have to cry? I thought of Dorothy in the *Wizard of Oz*, clicking her heels and going back home. I ached for that in that moment, to go back to our old house, to our old life, to not be in that bedroom, watching my dad—the strong, consistent, reliable, no-nonsense Dad—crying and hurting. And then I thought, *Was it me? Was I not good enough? Me, the accident, was I too much? Did I make them angry too many times with all my tattling or whining or fighting with my siblings?*

I can be better. I can do better, I wanted to say.

I can be quiet. I can go to bed on time and eat my vegetables. Would that help? Can I help? Please, please, Daddy, please don't leave.

■   ■   ■

In the therapy session, Joan shakes her head, Mom talks, and Dad sits so still and quiet. I want to fix them too. I want to make it all better for them now, just as I tried to do then. Because here I was again, causing the trouble.

When the silence permeates the room, Joan asks me, "Lee, how are you doing?"

"I am ashamed and embarrassed. I don't want them to think this is their problem."

"What does that feel like in your body?" Joan asks.

"I have no idea. It just hurts," I say.

"Lee, what if no one told you that you weren't good enough? What if your wiring just made you view things differently than the average person, and when you started your destructive coping skill of not eating, you couldn't stop? Even if you wanted to?" she asks me.

My Dad chimes in, "If anyone can get better, LeeWolfe, you can."

"Fine. Then why can't I do it now? Why can't I eat now?"

"Because you have years of emotions stuffed inside of you that you haven't expressed. And by not eating you are able to numb those out," Joan says.

"She has always been our emotional one; she has never been afraid to show her emotions," Mom says to the hippy-chick therapist.

"And I have a right to my own feelings," I say hard back to Mom. Joan scolds them, "It isn't your job to tell her how to feel."

We talk about it all in a very civil way, this family that doesn't talk about feelings. Dad and his late-night drinking. Mom and I and our chaotic relationship. We don't cry. We don't yell. It is polite and not "ugly," as Mom would say.

"My guess is there are some deep-seated emotions in there that need to come out," Joan says, and then she winks at me as if we have secret. We don't. But she is right. There are emotions like a rushing river flowing inside of me that, if I let out, I know I won't be able to stop or control.

And some of those emotions do erupt, not in the therapy session but after. Mom and I on a bench in the courtyard, my head hung low, her arm embracing me. "Why did you think you weren't good enough, Sweetheart? You know we love you."

"Mom, I don't know. I just don't know," I said, my anger boiling in me. I loved her, and she angered me in a way I couldn't describe. We started talking about the therapy session, and the voices began to rise as the tones became accusatory. "We love you so much. Don't you know that?" she asks.

"This isn't about love. This is about me. Me trying to just be me. You never have accepted me, always telling me to be someone else, to do something else, making fun of my 'Moonie group.' It never felt like it was enough or that I was enough."

We were now standing.

"I don't know where you get these crazy ideas," she says back.

"Why, Mom, why did you lie to me that day on the stairs? Why did you do that to Joe? All the lies and you sneaking off to 'tan' when you knew I knew!" I yelled.

"How dare you!" she says, fire in her eyes.

That same fire in my stomach.

"I have done nothing but support you and love you. All you can do is see my mistakes and judge me. Am I not good enough for you? Not the perfect mother you wanted? I did the best I could, and someday you will see that."

I said, between sobs, "Why can't you admit it now? Why?"

"My life is my business. I didn't raise you to be so disrespectful."

"No, your life is my business when it affects me."

We were inches away from each other. We yelled. We screamed, really. Both of us catching our breath between sobs. Who was right? Who was wrong? Who was hurt and who was the victim?

There wasn't an apology from either of us, but finally, what had been living between us was out. There was no magic wand making everything better. But for the first time I felt I had a voice. I could stand on my own two feet and say what I needed to. The validation didn't necessarily come from her, the validation came in therapy with my mini–Santa Claus therapist.

"What if all of your choices affected each other?" he asked me. "What if no one is to blame except all of you are to blame? That you are merely a family trying to make it through this journey called life, them merely parents who were actually trying to do their best with what they had, who sometimes didn't give you what you needed. What if they didn't know what you needed? And in the process, you didn't learn how to express your emotions or cope in a healthy way? Am I right?"

"Okay. So what do I do with that?" I asked.

"You stop blaming and look inside yourself. What do you need now to be fully you? To let go of what they thought of you or still think of you, and be the person you want to be?"

"I don't know," I said, unsure.

"Lee, what if life might change? Not because others change but because you can change your reaction to life. What if you let go of trying to change them and let them be who they were, the good *and* the bad?"

I took his words to heart, and very slowly, I began trying to understand, through lots of journaling and talking, who the person was underneath the eating disorder. Me, the Lee inside, was awakened in those offices.

After sessions, I returned to my jail, took the little pills and lived in the warm womb of my chair. I began to hate the EDU. I wanted to get out. I knew I had to behave, stop hiding my food, and sit in the chair and talk in groups if I wanted out.

There was a tiny sliver of a problem, though. I told myself I could have my eating disorder as a back up, just in case. *If things get too tough and you can't handle them, you can always numb out again. It is always an option.*

I knew what I wanted: I wanted to go back to Minnesota. I wanted to follow my dreams. I wanted space to find out who that person inside was that had been numb for so long. For the first time in many months, I picked up my Bible and started to read it again. The Lee inside of me began to remember, to put back together the parts of me that weren't the eating disorder. These parts of me loved to dance and sing and act silly. These parts of me weren't rigid and controlled. And these parts of me loved God and believed in something bigger than myself.

My voice, Lee's voice, began to hear the mean voices of the eating disorder, and I started saying, *Shut up, Ed!* When the voices got too strong, I picked up the phone and called Judy or Chris or Ashley. I talked with Judy and asked her if I could come back after I got out of the hospital.

"Lee," she said sweetly, "everyone misses you so much here. You are so loved. We want you to come back."

It was the love that gave me slivers of hope that there was

something else for me. God said he loved me because I was now reading it again. Others said that too. In everyone's attempt to do the right thing and say the right thing while I was so fragile, it was the love that kept me living—kept me believing. My parents, even if I didn't always see it, were saying "We love you, Lee. We will always love you." My sister, "I love you so much, Sister." My brother, "I love you, Twerp."

Even though, at the time, I didn't reflect this love back or acknowledge this love to them, it was their words of love that were my life raft.

pit

Set free. After many months, they opened the large doors, had me sign a sheet of paper, and I was out in the August heat. Under my arm was a blue three-ring binder filled with tools. Tools in the form of lots of papers with work I did while in treatment, meal plans, journals, artwork—things to fight the eating disorder. On my other arm was my brown duffle bag. Back in my white Toyota, I took that folder and threw it in the backseat.

Where it stayed untouched. Mistake number one.

My first stop was a convenience store where I giddily purchased a twenty-four-ounce Diet Coke. Happy and confident, I was the girl who stood on the podium that day so many years ago, believing the world was her playground. Finally free and able to do what I wanted, I drove out of Topeka as fast as possible as the tall clock tower disappeared in my rearview mirror: the hospital, the nurses, the craziness was in the past.

Minnesota and life were in my future.

That little problem I mentioned earlier? I hadn't given up Ed 100 percent. My fractured family was healing, but in my mind, Ed was there "just in case." Just in case things got tough again.

I knew Ed had to go, but I kept him in the back pocket for just in case. There for an emergency.

That is the biggest mistake I made that day after leaving treatment. While gripping the steering wheel, driving away as fast as possible, I thought: *Why and how would those people in that hospital have any idea how I am supposed to live? How I am supposed to cope? Did they have an eating disorder? Did they live my life? No. So why should I believe them? Telling me to follow a meal plan, to take medication, to follow the uncomfortable feelings in recovery. No, thank you, I was going to do it my way.*

By September I was in Minnesota, living in an obscenely large home as the live-in nanny. I was setting goals and rebuilding my life. Chris and I were spending time together again, reconnecting and repairing our relationship. I found a therapist named Jan and a psychiatrist named Dr. Groat. They were my treatment team.

I didn't listen to a word they said.

I acted well and smiled nicely. Everyone was happy; I was no longer causing trouble for them.

"You need to be taking medication," Dr. Groat would say as he leaned over his desk, a handsome man with a fit body, dark hair and one very messy office. We would spend most of our sessions arguing about the use of medication and why I, in all my wisdom, didn't think I needed medication.

"If God made me this way, then why should I take medication?" I would argue. "All it did for me in the hospital was make me sleep. I am creative and energetic. That is how God made me. I don't see why I should have to tamper with that to be what the world expects me to be."

He would be firm in his response, "Because you have a brain that doesn't connect all the synapses, Lee. You need the medication to make the connections. Plus, the medications they were prescribing you at the hospital, while not eating, was completely irresponsible and mismanaged. I am talking about low doses where you are monitored closely by someone who isn't misdiagnosing you."

Eyes rolling and hands thrown in the air, I would purchase the medications but let them sit on my bedside table, untouched. They grew in number as I filled various prescriptions yet refused to ingest them. Mistake number two.

And then there was the meal plan—or the lack of a meal plan. I assumed, with the amount of treatment I had gone through, I would naturally be able to eat again. To eat intuitively. Mistake number three.

I quickly learned we return to what we know, to what is most comfortable—even if that comfort destroys us.

Why would I return to not eating when I wanted to feel, wanted to live and wanted a life again? Because it was what I knew: it was a way to cope that was comfortable, familiar. I was comfortable in my discomfort. Even if it was slowly killing me. I couldn't see it happening.

I was pulling myself up by the bootstraps. *I can do this,* I thought. *I have already worked through the family stuff. I should be good to go.*

I didn't need anyone's help.

With Ed in my back pocket, as life began to seep its stress into my brain, I began to turn back to him. The descent into darkness started slow. Missing a meal here, working out a little more there. But with no accountability, the little lies took on a life of their own. My therapist, Jan, was an amazing Christian woman, and she was no fool. She would confront me, seeing right through my little games. So I hid more.

While Ed was my coping skill as I tried to find my voice again and fight, the depression was Ed's evil twin. Without medication and as I slowly began to lose weight again, sleep less and exercise more, the thoughts infected my head.

First, a shadow. Just a gray, shadowy film that filled my mind. Then it grew to dark clouds. Then I fell into the hole of sorrow. I was, for sure, not going to tell anyone. Why would I? Half a year spent in treatment, thousands of dollars out of my family's pockets, with relationships just beginning to be rebuilt. I was not going to share any of this with anyone. How could I put them through any more after all that time in the hospital? I should be well. Mistake number four.

The darkness overtook me and began to ooze into the marrow of my bones.

And God? I had prayed for healing. It wasn't happening. I was mad. Why wouldn't God heal me? Why wouldn't he set me free? Was I not worth it to him either? Did I not have enough faith? Was that why?

October 4, 1995

Dear Jesus,

This is it. I hope and pray that I don't go to hell. Also, that I don't fail. Goodbye.

Lee

I shut my worn, leather journal, full of my deepest thoughts, and I wrapped the thin strap tightly around it. I walked up the flight of stairs to my room in the attic. The people I worked for told me, "Make it your home." It was not my home. I was always envious of the girls in college who would escape on weekends to visit their childhood homes, homes where they had grown up and matured. Places to go back to. A base.

I didn't feel like I had ever really had a home—at least not a home that I lived in for more than a few years.

The stair rails were a deep mahogany and the walls a forest green, a less-than-cheery décor to match the prevailing mood in the house. As I turned the corner and walked up the narrow stairs to my room, my heart skipped a beat.

I had a secret.

It was *my* secret, and I felt euphoric to not be wavering on this decision anymore, a release to consider not having to fight this battle. No more obsessing about everything. No more of the stressful nanny job. No more sucking money out of my parents to take care of my problems. No more letters from friends asking how I was doing. No more people looking at me with those eyes of concern. No more.

My shaky hand grabbed the round, brass door handle, and I quickly opened the five-paneled door to the room provided for me. I tossed my journal onto the single bed, nuzzled tightly in the angled attic wall, and shut the door behind me.

Finally alone.

This enormous, brown stucco house in Minnesota was as dark on the inside as it was on the outside. When I first drove up to it a few months earlier in my clean, bright-white car, I wondered if I would be able to live in a place so dark. *It has to be better inside*, I thought.

It seemed like a dream job: live with a rich family in a big house, have my own room in the attic, hang out with the youngest daughter at the pool and perform some odd jobs around the house. Both of the parents were in intense, busy careers, and they were desperate for a nanny. I found out that they had a lot more in mind for me than I ever expected, much more than I was able to handle having just left a hospital. *I should*

*have known better. I should have had some boundaries. I should
have asked more questions.*

"I should haves." My life felt full of them.

Ed convinced me, *It isn't anyone's fault but your own. It will be
easier on everyone when you are gone. They can move on with their
lives. They won't have to worry about you anymore.*

I walked into my simple room: the single bed, neatly made
with my pink, floral, Laura Ashley bedspread, a white desk built
into the nook of the slanted wall, an old TV on a silver metal
stand, and a bathroom. I turned on the TV for noise. The walls
in my room were cream colored. Neutral. Boring. Lifeless. It was
how life had been these last three months. Neutral. Besides the
constant rage of thoughts about food and exercise, everything
else was dull. One simple day felt like too much; it was overwhelming. I needed it all to end.

I was done being neutral. I had been so good at it, feigning
friendships, pretending everything was better. My theater
training equipped me to appear like a happy twenty-three-year-
old nanny. I looked the part too, with my chin-length blond
bob, preppy clothes that were ironed meticulously with heavy
starch and a smile to finish it off. Always referred to as "the girl
next door" by my theater cohorts, most would never suspect the
turmoil churning inside my body. For the ones who did know, I
despised all the worry and pain I had brought them. It was
better if I played the part, acting like everything was okay.

My first therapist, the one who mostly talked about herself,
always encouraged me to use my acting skills. She told me
when I was stressed to think of another person I admired and
make the choices she would make. I tried it once. I spent an
entire day pretending I was Meg Ryan. For some reason, I felt
like Meg Ryan would go and eat ice cream, take her shoes off

and lie on the lawn. I am not sure why I imagined Meg Ryan would do that, but it sounded nice. So I purchased the largest scoop of ice cream I could find, took off my white Keds and laid my head on the green grass. For about fifteen minutes I envisioned my day as if I were Meg Ryan—shopping on Rodeo Drive, then going home to my mansion for a massage, after I stopped by my agent's office to pick up the new movie scripts being offered to me, of course.

It was a wonderful escape, until I got back into my little, white car—feeling bloated from all the ice cream I had eaten. I was suddenly back to myself and the same old obsessive thoughts began pumping through my brain: *Burn off the calories, burn off the calories. How am I going to burn off the calories?*

I walked to my organized closet and sat on the floor to sort my stuff. If I packed everything up, there would be no mess, easier for the people I was working for to manage. They could give my stuff to my friends and be done with me. I began putting everything in white plastic bins, labeling names on each. Behind my stomach, right beneath my ribcage, I felt a tightening of my muscles. I breathed in and tried to push the feeling out.

No hesitating, Lee. I continued my tasks. *I will leave my clothes for my sister.*

Sitting down at the little desk, I wrote letters to friends and family. And Chris. Chris could have my memory box where I saved our movie stubs, dried flowers and the love letters he had written me.

The muscles tightened, sending the ache to my back. *Breathe. Breathe.*

How will Chris take this? I don't want to hurt him, but I know he will be able to find someone better. A girlfriend without so many problems.

When I saw Chris earlier that day, he sensed something was different about me, maybe because it was the first time in a long time he had seen me happy and excited. I *was* happy, knowing it would all be over soon. The pain would be gone.

"Are you going to be okay tonight?" Chris kept asking. *Why did he ask me that?* I looked deeply into his big eyes and said, "Don't worry. I am fine. I love you." I leaned over the stick shift and kissed the side of his darkly tanned cheek, stepped out, shut the door to his car and walked into the mortuary of a house.

I hated lying to him. I hated every word as it came out of my mouth, but I knew I had to follow through with this. It had been too long, too many people burdened by my instability. It had to end.

I went in the tiny bathroom and turned on the brass faucet to wash my face. I grabbed onto the vanity with my right hand and leaned over to open the small window. The cool air rushed in and felt hard on my face. Goosebumps on my thin arms. Outside the window, the leaves were beginning to fall from overgrown oak trees. I hated October, with the chill in the air and the overcast sky. In Minnesota, October is the beginning of a long winter with little sun and lots of snow. And bitter cold.

The last Saturday Chris had taken me on a long car ride, sharing his love of nature and the outdoors. We drove up a winding dirt path to the top of a hill overlooking a forest, where he stopped the car in a small patch of grass. Most of the leaves had fallen, leaving the trees naked and exposed. He turned the car off and said, "Oh, look at these breathtaking colors and amazing smells."

I just felt cold and couldn't stop thinking about what to eat for dinner. Chris had opened the door and moved his powerful body out of the car. He walked to my side, opened my door and reached his thick arm in for me. My cold hand and bony wrist melted into his as our two hands touched, sending a tingle down to my toes. He helped me out of the car and we were standing kissing-distance away. He was large and warm next to me, protective and safe. My head was close to his neck and I was awash in the smell of his cologne and the warmth of his body. Together, hands still entwined, we walked forward for a better view. Leaves crunched under our feet, and quietly, in his deep voice, he persuaded, "Look at this, Lee. Isn't this beautiful? How can you be depressed when you are surrounded by so much beauty?"

I smiled politely and said, "Thanks for bringing me here; it is nice." Acting the part. Is that how Meg Ryan would talk to her boyfriend?

I didn't see beauty. I saw cold and pain, death and loneliness.

I looked in the mirror and continued to grip the cold edges of the linoleum sink. Sky blue eyes stared back at me, unforgiving. I didn't know whose they were. Who was this woman, this shell of a person? And where did she go? What a fake I was. What a failure. What a disappointment I had been, to God, to everyone.

I saw nothing behind the eyes—nothing left but empty blue stones between my eyelids.

I felt my heart quicken and my tummy clench with an overwhelming desire to hurt, to feel, to be alive one last time. My right hand grabbed the pink razor perched on the vanity and quickly slashed at my left wrist. The left hand released its hold on the vanity and I slashed it again. Again.

Pain.

Numb.

Hot.

I began to brush my teeth. My left arm tingled as drops of

blood fell onto the neutral carpet. I deserved this. I deserved to be punished. I deserved this pain—for all the pain I had caused everyone. I could hear my parents' voices, like they were right there with me, forgetting so quickly all the healing that had been happening between us: *Too much, too much. Slow down, Lee. Quit overexaggerating. You're so overdramatic. You are just too much . . .*

The burden my life has caused them really has been too much. They must have been right, I thought. I set the toothbrush on the vanity, then filled a clear plastic cup with water, turned the faucet off and walked back into my room. I placed the cup next to the bed and returned to my closet. My pink pajama pants and white T-shirt were neatly folded on top of my boxes. I changed into them, folded up the clothes from the day, set them gently back on the boxes and turned off the light to the closet to walk toward my bed. I noticed the TV show, an old black-and-white rerun of *I Love Lucy.*

This pity party was over. I may have done lots of things wrong in my life, but I could at least do this right. I sat on the side of my bed where the antidepressants and antianxiety pills pre-scribed by my psychiatrist were waiting for me in the tiny night-stand. I didn't want these pills when I got out of the hospital. I was tired of being medicated. But day by day they sat, patiently waiting in the drawer, for "just in case."

I wrapped my hands around the three large bottles of pills. I leaned my head back and poured a few pills down my throat. Picked up the glass and drank.

I shut my lips together and swallowed them down.

Drink. Pour.

One bottle gone.

Drink. Pour.

More . . . more . . .

Drink. Pour.

That has to do it.

I thought of Chris. I thought of God. I thought of Lucille Ball and the way she made people laugh.

Warmth quickly took over my body, and my eyelids felt heavy. I could see Lucille Ball laughing and giggling as she jumped around. The audience's laughter sounded like it was coming out of a can. Lucy's giggle echoed in my head, almost sinister.

Was she laughing at me?

Was I laughing at me? Who was that laughing?

Maybe it was God laughing?

It hurt my ears. Too much. Life was too much. I couldn't do it anymore.

It will be over soon, Ed whispered. My body relaxed and my eyelids grew heavier and heavier.

I prayed one last time: *Please forgive me, God. Please, don't send me to hell.*

19

the fight

Piercing sirens shot through my ears, forcing every part of me to wake up. I felt a sharp pinch in my left arm. *Someone is sticking a pencil in me. Why would they want to poison me with lead?*

I aimed to turn my head, but it weighed too much. My skull so heavy, so thick and full.

I slowly rolled my lead-filled, bowling-ball head to the left and saw a man in a dark blue shirt with dark blue pants examining my left arm. Then I saw him inserting a tube.

The earsplitting sirens were about to shatter my ears, and I knew my head was going to explode.

Where the hell am I? I could feel movement like I was on a school bus and I heard the sirens, but where was I? *What happened? Why was my heart banging out of my chest?*

I didn't understand. I just wanted to go to sleep forever. Why was this guy in the blue clothes keeping me awake, infecting me with lead and hurting me with the deafening noise?

I drifted back to my ocean, the blue behind my eyes, the quiet in my head. It was calm. It was light. It was peaceful and overwhelmingly beautiful. Just me and the waves, the light whoosh of the ripples coming to the shore. The smell of clean, crisp, fresh morning air. Me, somewhere between the waves and the air.

Like a newborn baby slapped into this world, I was smacked back awake with a long tube being inserted into my throat.

I couldn't breathe.

The taste of something thick and dark began to fill me. With a powerful force, I felt the tar push into my stomach and clog my body.

Tar. Someone is filling me with tar.

My worst nightmare had come true.

I am in hell. This is what hell is: a place where they fill you with lead and tar.

But something wasn't right because Chris was there. He was standing somewhere in the room. I felt him there and then saw him. His hands in his jean pockets, his black hair sticking every different way, and his brown eyes swollen and puffy. *What is he doing in hell?* The tar and the suctioning made me gag, and I couldn't breathe again.

I wanted to scream, "Leave me alone! Stop torturing me! Haven't I been tortured enough? Let me be!"

I was pulled toward the weight of Chris and his eyes. I knew I loved him. I felt him loving me in this room. He just stared at me, his big coffee eyes, thick with concern and wonder and pain. *Why does he look so sad? Maybe I took him to hell with me and he doesn't want to be there?*

As I stared at him, a woman in a green matching outfit lifted up a pair of blue scissors and brought them toward me.

First the lead and tar, now scissors.

She held the scissors on my pink T-shirt and began to cut right down the center. I could feel the cold, hard scissors against my skin. She pulled both sides of my T-shirt open to expose my naked chest to the room full of torturers.

I saw Chris turn his head, trying to be respectful.

And then it hit me. This was worse than hell . . . they were keeping me alive!

The white walls, the smell of hydrogen peroxide, the people in scrubs, I had been there before. I knew where I was. *Oh no. Oh God, I was back in a hospital. Again.*

What happened? Who found me? Why didn't they let me die? I thought I planned it perfectly. I thought I took enough pills. Why didn't it work? Oh my God, what if they called my parents? My body and mind demanded I scream, and I struggled to scream when the shaking set in. My body an earthquake, shaking the room, the walls, the people, everything shaking. I felt my body rolling from side to side. "Don't call my parents," I heard myself yell. "Don't call my parents. . . . Don't call my parents!" I wanted this tube out of my throat so I could scream louder, so they could hear me scream, "Please, don't call my parents."

"Calm down," one of the torturers says.

"Calm down," another one whispered and touched my arm. The tar filled my veins, my stomach and my body tight.

Scream.

Scream. Scream louder.

This is hell. I am in hell. I want to die. Why won't they let me die? My heart began to beat out of my chest again. The green nurse put something cold between my exposed breasts. There was no hiding here, no masking, no pretending. I was naked, frightened out of my mind, angry, alone. This was worse than hell; it was living hell.

■　　■　　■

Later I learned what happened on the night of the attempt. Chris was awake most of the night. Worried. He called Jan, called friends. "No real evidence, just a sense," he told them, "a sense that something is wrong with Lee."

I had called Ashley to thank her for being such a great friend, which had her concerned. Yet most told Chris, "Wait until morning."

But he couldn't. He couldn't wait. He was alert and stirring, wondering. He finally left his house while the sun began to rise. He had called to the home where I was living. "Go check on Lee," he said.

"Why?" the mother asked.

"Something isn't right. Something is wrong," he pleaded.

They said they would. They didn't.

He had the sense, "a nudging from God," he said. So he drove. Fast. To the home with the dark outside. To find me.

Banging on the door, they came slowly.

"Did you check on her? Is she okay?" he asked the mother, standing behind the door.

"No, not yet."

He didn't reply but ran. Busted through the doors and ran through that house, up three flights of stairs to my room. He burst through the door and found me, lying on the floor in a pool of vomit.

"Call 911," he screamed. "Call 911!"

"Had he not come, had you been there longer, you might have died," they told me. "A miracle."

■ ■ ■

The room spun around and around like the spinning rides I loved as a kid, and I held my arms close to the sheets to keep my body from wobbling. *Stare at the light, Lee. Dive into it.* My body hurt; it burned. I didn't care. I deserved it. I closed my eyes and, when they closed, I saw dark with a faint spot of light behind the darkness. The light spun too, though not in one spot like you sometimes see right behind your eyes after looking at a bright light, but everywhere. Eventually sleep rescued me. But this sleep—maybe it was all night or maybe a fifteen-minute snooze, I am not sure—changed me forever.

Because there was a battle in my room. At the end of my bed, actually.

They stood behind the metal bed and they fought violently. I saw them fighting, but I couldn't make out who *they* were. There was gray dust everywhere. And I was there in between them, standing. My throat no longer burned, and my body wore different clothes, ones that weren't ripped. But they were ripping me, tearing me apart like a piece of paper. There were two sides: one side pulled my right arm and the other my left. I was unfazed and unfeeling. Not happy. Not sad.

"Take me," I yelled. "Take me." They pulled, and I was thrown around, back and forth with my head whipping from side to side. Dust filled the room, making it difficult to see what was happening. And just like it happens in tug of war, when the winners triumph and the rope explodes full force over to the winning side, I fell onto the triumphant side in open space. It felt as if I was falling out of a fifty-story window, screaming the entire way down, my body flailing every which way—free and boundaryless until the soft, warm landing caught me. Right before I settled into the landing, I woke up.

Two nurses had my arms, holding me down. *Was I throttling my body in bed while I slept? Is that why they came to hold me down? Or was it just coincidence they were there? Was it them pulling me?* I breathed in, the air cold and stale, and let it out. The memory of this dream didn't come back to me until a few days later. I was out of the ICU where the dream happened and back in another mental ward—this time in Minnesota. No longer interested in creating a student council here, no longer wanting to make friends, I stayed in my room alone.

But that dream? What was that dream? Did it happen? Three days later, it still felt real to me. I wondered if it was a medication or drug-induced haze. I did take a large amount of pills that night. But do you know what I really think? I think it was a battle for my soul. At the end of my bed there was God and there was Satan, and they were fighting for me. I felt it.

Yet I was confused when I woke up, because there was still a part of me that felt like I was living in hell, that I would have been better off dead. I tried to reason with myself, but I only came up with reasons why being alive was the worst place to be. *Well, let's see. I can, in fact, offer many reasons why: Not only do my friends and family not trust me because of my eating disorder, now I am a danger to myself. And if I am a danger to myself, then am I a hazardous accessory to any others that choose to hang with me? Why yes. One person in particular, really. Chris.*

Chris was there while I was in the ICU, but then he left. Out of town on a spontaneous camping trip with his dad. Man to man, they would talk about this crazy girl he was dating, and his dad will tell him to run. Fast. "What if you marry her and she kills herself? What if you have children and she starves them? What kind of future can you have with this woman?" he asked Chris while loons whistled in the background, the two of them warming their hands over the fire. "Is that what you want for your life?"

And my parents. They did come. In fact, my mom and my dad's girlfriend, Debbie, drove seven hours together to see me lying in a hospital bed, my body frail like a starving child. How was I to face them?

I wondered what I would do. Who was going to hire someone with a nice mental record, including a suicide attempt? And then there was a place to live. Where would I go? I sure couldn't return to the house I tried to take my own life in. Somehow my things were returned to me, but the family I worked for never visited, never called, never spoke to me ever again. And how about going back to Kansas? I didn't want to go back to Kansas.

I thought about my community, my army: Brad, Ashley, Brooks, Deb and Dana, all of them together in the waiting room, praying for me. Crazy me. How could I face them? I remember all the people who came to visit. They looked down at me in bed, their eyes sad, my choice hurting them deep. Would they let me back in?

I spun the thoughts and remembered again about the fight at the end of my bed, and I wondered, *Who actually won that day? Was it God? Or was it Satan?* Only time would tell, and at this point I had plenty of it.

What did I know for sure? A mental hospital would not help me. I had the tools; they were in a blue folder in the back of my car. They sat there unopened because I was too stubborn to use them. *Do I want to now? Is this it?* I said to myself, *Is this what is finally going to get you to listen to what those helping you are trying to say?*

Right there was my voice. I began to hear. It was quiet, and it was mad. Mad that I didn't give it room, didn't give it space. I heard it telling me to make a choice, make a choice between death and life. God wasn't making that choice at the end of the bed; I was. I was choosing death every time I gave into the eating disorder and believed its lies. Eating disorders are not choices, but recovery is.

20

the choice

The thoughts were crawling all over me now, and I couldn't smash any of them, couldn't find my center in the midst of all of it. I got out of bed and walked down the narrow corridor and found a coffee station carved out in a wall. Styrofoam cups, Coffee-Mate coffee maker and Sweet'N Low. Same at every hospital. Same bitter taste. I swallowed it down and leaned against the wall in the hallway. It was quiet, except for the whispers and giggles of conversation at the nurses station a few feet away. I didn't want to talk to anyone, so I took my coffee and went back to my room at the end of the hall. The green vinyl chair squeaked as I sat in it, and I found my journal, the same one I'd written in before I swallowed the pills.

October 7, 1995

Lord,

Alive. Another day. A gift. Why do I not see the gift? Sometimes it seems like all the prayers in the world don't help me if I can't believe in myself. I don't care to live. I don't care to go on. I don't want to live a suicidal life like this. I wish they wouldn't have found me. I wish I was asleep on that floor. But, God, that is not

from you. I know . . . then why don't I want to try life again? I
am pouring this out to you in complete honesty. Why didn't my
heart stop? Why didn't I die? I don't enjoy, life, people, laughter.
I am always afraid of abandonment. It is too much. God, please
hold my hand when I walk in that house. I am scared. I feel so
bad for hurting everyone. Who would ask me to babysit now?
Everyone knows now. I feel so stupid. Why are you keeping me
here? And what do you mean, "Those who wait on the LORD
Shall renew their strength; They shall mount up with wings like
eagles They shall run and not be weary, They shall walk and not
faint" (Isaiah 40:31)?

Lee

I drank the coffee and looked down at my legs tucked underneath me. Sticks. Mere sticks those legs of mine. I went back to
the voice telling me to make a choice. To try life. Not halfway
but fully participate in it, without running to a coping skill that
would leave me numb. A coping skill that might not leave me
alive. I thought about this idea. Maybe God was speaking to me.
Maybe God had been there all along, but it was me who wouldn't
participate, give up control, fully surrender. Was God healing
me, but I didn't want to be healed? There were places in the
Bible where he asked people, "Do you want to be healed?"
Couldn't recall where exactly, but I knew he did.

Lee, do you want to be healed?

I felt those words press against my skull, and I recalled a
pool. Yes, it was a pool. That guy in the Bible was lying by a pool
for many years, waiting to get well. I remembered my Young
Life leader Jill telling the story. Standing in a cramped room in a
basement, this petite woman with a sandy blond bob and an
amazing amount of energy told this story of the man who was
lying by the pool on a mat. Jesus came by and asked him if he

wanted to get well. The man started whining and complaining about all of his friends, how he was waiting for them to put him in the pool because the pool was going to heal him, but they didn't, so he waited.

Was I him, waiting by the pool, dipping my big toe in and pulling it back out because of the cold water? Jesus said to him, "Pick up your mat and walk" (John 5:8).

Oh yeah, it came back to me. The man was crippled and couldn't get into the pool. Jesus heals him then, and the paraplegic by the pool picks up his mat and walks.

This story made me cry. Hard. Sobbing hysterically, so much so that I was unable to catch my breath. The coffee cup still gripped in my hand, the rest of me spinning. Words ran like a wild herd of animals through my mind. Words and images of the past few years, and I couldn't catch my breath. I knew what was happening, this gripping on my heart, this sucking in of air like it was coming through a tiny straw. A panic attack. The emotions flooded me so fast my body couldn't keep up, so it fought by panicking.

I moved onto my knees, my elbows on the scratchy sheets, my forehead hanging on the mattress, my eyes on the tile floor trying to find something to focus on. A dust bunny, a speck in the floor, anything. I prayed out loud, "God, this is it. I am willing, God. Willing to give this thing up. One hundred percent. God, I know I have said this before."

I had. Many times, I had prayed for God to heal me, to take this cup from me, to rescue me.

The question now wasn't "Will God heal me?" The question was "Do I want to be healed?"

Yes.

Really, I had no other option. I could continue to do what I was doing, the starving, the overexercising, the filling my schedule with too much. I could do that and think it was going to work this time. Maybe it would. But maybe it wouldn't. And maybe the next time there would not be a Chris to come banging on the door. Or a doctor to pump the drugs out. There might not be a next time. And, what if? What if there was hope? What if God had a plan like it says in the Bible? What if I believed God had a plan and leaned into it? What would that look like?

Not an option. The words came to me. *Ed, not an option. I have to choose another option.*

Didn't I hear somewhere that insanity is doing the same thing over and over again, expecting a different result each time? "Today I have given you the choice between life and death, between blessings and curses. Now I call on heaven and earth to witness the choice you make. Oh, that you would choose life, so that you and your descendants might live!" (Deuteronomy 30:19 NLT).

Ed. Not an option.

"God, I surrender. Yours. I am yours. You win, God. I give this to you. I can't do it anymore, and I need you to show me the way. Show me the steps to take. Show me how to live the life you have planned *without* the eating disorder," I said aloud.

And then I got a bit picky with God.

"But, if in a year, I don't feel any better or different, if within a year of trying it your way I am not better . . . then I am coming back to Ed."

I knew you weren't supposed to make deals with God, but that was my offer. Take it or leave it. He took it.

Now the ball was in my court to do what was required of me.

What happened that day wasn't some special connection or magical prayer. What happened was that someone died that day.

That someone was *not* me.

October 12, 1995

Discharge from Dr. Groat. He states he agrees with my recommendation not to pursue inpatient with Lee. Discussed impressions of Dr. Richardson that client was almost "overprotected" at Menninger and, in fact, learned how to cut and self-mutilate. Discussed my plan and that she would continue either with Dr. Groat or possibly work with Dr. Richardson.

October 16, 1995

Patient is able to function because of her own strength and her faith in God. States she feels little support from Chris and her friends, and is unsure of her relationship with Chris. Discussed elements of that relationship which are unhealthy, as well as healthy aspects. Discussed the battle she was engaged in with death and affirmed her victory over life. She states she believes she won the battle but would like some support. Discussed sources of support, as well as realistic expectations as to how much others can give to her. Evaluates where she has been and where she is going. Reports feeling overwhelmed by where to go next and so we "chunked" out areas to begin: first, find a permanent place to live and, second, begin to volunteer. Assessment: feels disappointed by Chris and friends that they aren't supportive enough. Appears still fragile yet with some symptoms of strength in herself and beginning to trust our relationship. Plan: she will not exercise until doctor's appointment in two weeks. Will contact a nutritionist at Fairview. Will move slowly to find an apartment.

Reports she is glad to be alive.

Jan Zahner, MSW, LCSW

■   ■   ■

While in the hospital, Judy told me of a friend of hers from church who said I could live in her basement until I was back on my feet again. I had no other options, so I said yes. It was a room with pink and green flowers all over the walls. She sat across from me, her hair curled perfectly and in very crisp clothes, and she talked to me but didn't talk to me. It was as if she was talking *at* me—her sweetness a little too sugary. I was surprised she wasn't wearing a headband.

"Welcome, you are so welcome here," she said.

Her husband was around every so often, but mostly it was her. And me.

I slept stiff under those scratchy, flowery covers. A smell in the air made it hard for me to relax. Too much perfume. Too many flowers. I bumbled around in bed, thinking and wondering about the weird sensation in this home. It felt like they were trying to mask what was underneath, masking the fear. A girl living in their basement. A girl who might try to kill herself again. What would that look like, having the ambulance at their beautiful home in their fancy neighborhood? Would that look like a reflection on her?

I was no longer a girl who struggled to eat. I was now a girl who struggled to live. And for those around me, I was like a walking yellow caution tape. I noticed the hesitation in conversation, the eyes that now held drops of fear in them. I saw it now in everyone who knew me. How could I blame them? I couldn't explain myself. I had no words to explain the deep, dark horrible pit that I had been in. How could I explain that I was beyond myself? And in a Christian community, how would I explain that, yes, I do love God, and yes, I did want to die. Wasn't that the sin above of all sins? Taking away the life that God had given me? Destroying the body that God had given me?

I realized that for me to acknowledge the vulnerability of these feelings would possibly mean that others might have to acknowledge that, yes, they too might sometimes feel that way. I realized, for most people, it is easier to point and stare, to say, "I am not like that! I am not like *her!*" Or, "You are the crazy one!" And that is what she did, the lady with the pink and green and the smelly perfume.

I came and went, I made my bed, and I quietly tiptoed through the house. But her fear overwhelmed her, and she only said out loud exactly what I already knew—exactly what I already saw in the eyes.

"You have to leave. I can't have you here," she told me.

There was no real reason except: I couldn't stay. Her eyes wide and falsely compassionate, like she had looked in the mirror and practiced. I left as quickly as I had come. I packed up my leather duffle bag and drove away. I drove my car to an empty lot and stared out the window. Where would I go now? Where would I stay? My breath, now shallow and my tears rushing strong, "Why, God? Why, God? Why did you make me!" I screamed, "Why, God? What am I supposed to do now?" I looked up into the gray, fuzzy interior of my car, and I screamed a deep and thick scream.

"Help me, God. Help me. You kept me alive. For what? For this? For more pain?" And then my fists hit. Hit the steering wheel over and over, as I cried and screamed until my voice had nothing left.

I was exhausted. I was petrified. I was alive, and I wasn't numb. *Do the next right thing,* I heard a voice say. Do the next right thing? Then I heard, *I got this. Trust me.* Whatever the next right thing was, it led me back to comfort. As much as I dig in my memory, I don't know how it happened, the conversations or the asking. All I know is shortly after this, I was at Dave and Judy's—back in the room with the trophies.

Allowing me to stay in their home again was the lived-out version of grace. I didn't see the fear in their eyes—or at least they didn't show it. I knew they had fear about having me there. I knew they also had to wonder if I would do it again, if they would find me like Chris did, in a pool of vomit. Yet they somehow put their own unease aside. They saw me; underneath the pain and the eating disorder, they saw me. And that was spark enough for me to believe that, yes, maybe there was hope. Maybe God did have a plan.

one day at a time

I focused on the race. One year. God and I had a deal, a covenant. If there was one thing I strived to be, it was a woman of my word, just like Dad was. I wanted to prove to God that I would fulfill my end of the bargain.

It was like driving blind—literally like getting in the car, fumbling around the key entry and then pressing the gas, hoping you don't hit anyone. But before you know it, maybe two or three seconds into the drive, you bump something, run over something, run into something. Then you stop and try again. And again. And again.

I would get up early, pray and then scribble frantically in my journal about my anxieties—attempting to release them on a page. Then I would walk downstairs into the kitchen, assemble my breakfast while reading the slip of paper that held my meal-plan chart. I found it in the binder of my blue book from Menninger and also brought it to my sessions with my dietitian. It became my constant measuring stick of success. It used to be a game to see how many empty spaces I could leave. Now it was a game to see how perfectly I could do the meal plan. It wasn't normal eating, like walking into the kitchen and picking what you want; I couldn't do that yet. I needed it written out for me, what I was supposed to have. It was lines on a page, reflecting back to me what was accomplished that day. The goal now was not numbness. The goal was living.

I had no choice. Ed was not an option.

So what is *brave*? Brave is climbing Mount Everest. Brave is speaking in front of thousands of people. Brave to me did not equate to eating a hot dog or pizza. Or did it? Because that is what brave became for me. *Brave* and *fear* became words that saturated my days. Long days of reclaiming a life that was stolen—stolen first by depression and then by Ed. The covenant was made, and I was willing, willing to give recovery a try.

Why was I willing now, now when I had nothing left? No job. Disappointed family. Disillusioned friends. Lacking health. No college degree. Yet God had grabbed my heart in that hospital and I was finally willing. I realized that surrender only happens when one is fully willing to surrender—in my case, at least for a full year.

Was it because *he* won the fight at the end of my bed? Was it because I finally let go? Or was it because of the excessive amount of prayers from those on the sidelines who were watching me destroy myself? I don't know. All I know is I was finally in the battle, ready to fight.

No other option. The other option was death.

And, by the grace of God, I was given a second chance. I now know that God wants that for everyone. So the brave steps of climbing back into life and out of the pit began.

Mornings at the center island. The house was quiet. I slowly ate my cereal and my yogurt, and drank my juice in the required amount. I repeated these words in my head: *Ed, not an option. I have to find another option.* Spoon in my mouth, and then I would chew: one, two, three. Swallow. My stomach offered me no signals of full or hungry, as we were not yet friends. I would stare at the white sheet of paper for tallies of food groups and mark them with my pencil. Ed would whisper, *Don't do it.*

I would say back, *I will do it anyway. Even when I don't want to.*

Breakfast done. *Fuel in. That is all it is, Lee. Fuel. You don't think about the gas when you put it in the car, why do you think about the food? It is just food.*

Ed told me calories. I told Ed to shut up.

I stared out the kitchen window, leaves gone. The winter coming and a shiver crawled down my spine. A shiver of fear. I said out loud: "Life. I choose life."

These words of life began to take on a powerful meaning for me. I realized, when washing my dishes from my morning fuel, that every time I marked a tally on my sheet I was making one step closer to life. I was alive. I was breathing. There must have been a reason. Wasn't there? So if I continued to make more choices each day toward *life* and less choices toward death, then maybe I could actually claw out of this living hell?

The charting and obsessiveness took over, but this time, it wasn't in miles run or lack of calories eaten: it was in the game of life versus death.

I ate my breakfast. One mark for life.

I didn't go on a run to make up for the calories. Another life point.

I spent fifteen minutes in prayer. Life was winning.

I took my medication. Ding. Life has a lead here.

I contemplated crawling into bed and chose to call Chris instead. Yep, that helps too.

It became a game. I had the skills, I realized, after a few weeks of playing. The same skills I used to get me into my eating disorder, when applied toward fighting my eating disorder, served me well.

So the day to day consisted of this minutiae in the life game: asking myself if it was a choice toward life or one toward death. I realized it was a black-and-white way of thinking, but it worked for me. Death was pulling me, yanking on me, begging me to return to it. I knew the master of that seeking me out was the evil one, masked as the eating disorder.

I knew it would lead me back to the dark place. I knew that dark place led me nowhere. I had told God I would give this thing called *life* a try. So I was.

Everything I did in those few weeks after the hospital were built on this verse, "'For I know the plans I have for you,' says the LORD. 'They are plans for good and not for disaster, to give you a future and a hope'" (Jeremiah 29:11 NLT).

Two things happened to prove to me that life was changing: tears and laughter.

The eating disorder, for me, was a result of refusing to feel. "You can't expect to numb out pain and not numb out joy. They are friends," Jan would say. So in choosing life, I began to have tears—a substantial amount of tears. Some days the life game felt too hard. Lying in my bed at the Carvers', I would look at the room still filled with Jayhawk posters, photos, and Edina green-and-white memorabilia all around me on the white shelf at the top of his room. Reminders of his happy life of living. Not my life. Not my room. I had no room like this. My reminders were cuts on my arm and sad faces from my family. My reminders were in a box in a basement in Kansas. So I'd curl under the down comforter, hide and cry.

Some days, very simple things set me off—like the sounds of the school bus. The whine of the engine as it trudged up the hill, the squeaking gears when it turned the corners, it triggered a flood of emotions. Reminded me of the school bus on the day Dad said, "We will have a family meeting tonight." The school bus, back when I was nannying, standing on the street, helping the kids to school for their day. And then thinking about the doctor's piercing words in the hospital only a few weeks earlier: "The damage you have done to your body might be so great to cause you to not ever have children. Only time will tell. But this is a real possibility for you, Lee." That put me into a frenzy of sobs.

"And your heart, very fragile right now, after all it has been through. You will be lucky if you can make it around the three miles of Lake Harriet."

Exercise wasn't allowed yet. My body, fragile. My soul, fragile. My heart, bruised and beaten.

But God heals hearts. God repairs them. And once I was in the game of life, the heart surgery began.

The agony of trying to get up out of bed and participate was really the hardest part. After hearing the school bus and the silence in the house, I would be awash in sadness.

Yet the days I participated, did things that brought joy and made plans with friends, I found laughter again. Before, when I was socializing, there was always this part of me somewhere else. The Ed part was over in a corner of my mind, calculating calories or reminding me to be cautious. When I started letting go of Ed and choosing life, there was real communication and real laughter. I would sit with Ashley and Deb, eat pizza, and laugh and talk. And it began to feel normal because I was present.

My therapist, Jan, consistently asked me, "This is your life. What do you want to do with it?"

"Therapeutic relationships can be gateways to real living, but you need to participate," Jan would remind me. I had participated at Menninger, but in the back of my mind, I still hung onto the idea that I had Ed. This time, I was fully honest. Fully me. And it scared me from the top of my head right down to underneath my toenails.

I sat in her small office with Jan in her swivel chair, her desk behind her piled with paper. The office smelled like fresh flowers, but not in the ghastly sweet way, and that is all I remember. I can't remember what she wore or how she sat or even pictures on the walls. But I remember her eyes: tender, warm and gentle. I trusted her.

She listened, she sometimes cried with me, and she never gave up hope. I would come in and tell her about the game of life I was playing. She told me it was working.

"How?" I said. "Am I fat now? Is that why it is working?"

"No," she said, not taking the eating disorder's bait. "It is your eyes. I see it in your eyes."

"What do you see in my eyes?"

"A brightness. A hunger. You are hungry for life. I see it in your eyes."

"How? How can you see that?"

"I see it."

She was right. There was a hunger for life. Standing on that cliff of death, I began to wonder if I could be set free. I was up for the challenge.

The other piece that was helping, without me knowing it, was my meal plan. By beginning to follow the meal plan, for the first time, things were happening to me inside. Mostly the feelings were happening again because, by eating, my brain was working, my mind was fresher, and I was no longer in a perpetually numb state of hunger. The feelings were confusing and baffling and hard to define at times, but they were emerging. Many of them landed on the berber carpet of Jan's office or wadded in balls of Kleenex left in her trash, but they were happening. I began to feel my feet on the ground.

That same day Jan told me about the brightness in my eyes she asked me another question. The silence in the room made me uncomfortable, and she leaned forward and looked at me hard: "Who are you doing recovery for, Lee?"

"I don't know."

"Yes, you do. You know." She continued, "Are you doing it for Chris? Your dad? Your mom?"

I couldn't answer that. I avoided the question and moved to another topic. "I need a job," I told her.

But that question was a crucial one that is still helpful to this day: *Who am I doing recovery for?* Well, if I looked back, when I ate the food at Menninger, it was out of shame, pure embarrassment that I couldn't eat the simplest food. So I did it anyway, so I could say to Dad, "I ate a hamburger today. Aren't you proud of me?" Or tell Mom, "I am doing really great. I had ice cream today, and it was really good."

Total lies.

I hated every minute of it, and all I could think about then was the calories—adding them over and over in my head. I wanted approval from my parents. Wanted *some* sort of approval for *something.* I wanted them to tell me I was good enough, I mattered. I was searching in the wrong place.

Jan continued, "If you do recovery for someone else, it can't last. It just can't. External motivation only works for so long. It works for a little bit, and can be the steps you need to take to get you moving, but ultimately it can't last." Jan knew what she was doing.

Who was I doing recovery for?

She followed up with, "If you never get the approval from them that you are looking for, then what?"

I had to seek the Source. The one who knit me together.

I had to do recovery for one person: God. Because I had faith that was growing again, I had renewed faith that God's words meant what they said—that he knew the plans he had for me. The striving and the trying to be someone I wasn't meant to be was getting me nowhere. I needed to do recovery in spite of everyone. I had to radically accept the fact I might not ever, might never get the approval from my family that I was looking for. The approval that said it was okay to be the person I was in our broken family system.

And I had to let it go. Let go of the striving that had been happening since I was twelve years old—striving to fix. To fix my Dad's drinking. To change my Mom into the mom I wanted. To not be the person I was. To be the person they wanted me to be. I had to let it go.

And that decision was another one, freeing me into a world of living, a world where I began to dream again, to believe again, to see a future again.

March 8, 1996

Dear Ed,

First of all, you are ugly and I don't like you. Your name is ugly. Second, you buddy up with the devil and I don't like him. There is no room for him in my life. You know why? Because I have a better friend. His name is Jesus. He never changes. He created me for good and wants me here on earth. If he didn't, he would have let you take me in October. He blesses me with special friends and surrounds me with love. Sometimes he shows up in weird ways, but I can always count on him. You try and whisper negative thoughts in my ear and tell me to stay alone. But Jesus can whisper and his voice STILL out-speaks your voice. You make me think being skinny or being numb will bring happiness. Or being #1 at everything will bring happiness. But that keeps me from friends and from love. I know the word *love* makes you sick. To love myself would leave no room for you. I will no longer let you tell me to abuse myself, to starve myself, to binge or to overexercise. I am not going to obey you. God wants me to set my mind on *his* thoughts and *his* words to enjoy life. I am not here to worship you. You are mean and hurtful. You make my parents worry, clog my mind and keep me a child. Screw off. You have no power in my life. I have the power of the Holy Spirit. He is loving, forgiving and everlasting. I can't worship you both. So, GO AWAY and leave me alone.

Lee

elephant in the room

We were meeting his family for dinner. It was the first time I had been with them since the hospital—his sister, his mom, his dad—and we were all meeting at a restaurant downtown. I had met his parents before. They were warm and kind and full of long, tight hugs.

There was fear in his silence. I knew it. As we drove downtown, the laughter, the chatter, the conversation was absent. I knew what was going on. Chris wondered what they would say to me. Or maybe he wondered what I would say to them. Fresh off my encounter with God in the hospital, I loved sharing the story of God winning the fight for my soul.

"Don't tell people that story," Chris would say. "It freaks them out."

"No, it freaks you out," I would reply.

"No, it is just such a deep and intense story; not everyone can relate to it. It is your experience, and not everyone can relate."

It was his parents he was referring to. He *was* scared. He had every right to be. How could I blame him, really? Wasn't he the fool for sticking around? Weren't people thinking that? And his parents—Unitarian Universalists—what would they think of my story with images of God and the devil and hell and my soul? No, not appropriate dinner conversation.

"Why don't you just say what is going on?" I finally blurted out.

"What are you talking about?"

"This silence. Your silence. You are afraid, aren't you? Afraid of what they will say. What they will think. Not about that story but about me, about what I did."

"Yes," he said.

A kick in the gut. He was right. That response was normal, and they had every right to be concerned. Did I know if I would do it again? Did I know if I would recover? Was I a safe person to continue in a relationship with? I didn't know. I couldn't guarantee that for him.

During this time, I was doing everything possible to move forward in recovery. One very helpful tool was attending a support group led by my therapist, Jan. It was a place where I could sit with others and share my struggles to "eat a tally." Or say something was "triggering." And they would shake their heads, nod and say, "Oh yeah, me too!" This group was not necessarily my everyday community but rather a support system that could speak the language of the eating disorder and help me through.

That same week in group, we had discussed the issue of family and friends, and how they dealt with the illness. I was aware of Chris's family's and friends' hesitations about me. A few of his friends had even encouraged him to start reaching out, to try dating again while I was in the hospital—encouraging him to move on. I wasn't naive to their misgivings about me and my struggles, and I knew it wasn't my job to prove anything to them. But still, it hurt deeply.

My everyday community continued to be made up of my Young Life friends, and I also began to make new friends at the church we were attending. The friends who had been with me on this journey still had fear in their eyes, but I knew I had caused it. We spent time hanging out at my friend Deb's house, who I had met my first night in Minnesota, at that bar with Chris. Deb and Brooks cried for me, and for their own pain too. Deb later shared with me that, by seeing what I went through, she realized that perfection was not worth it. It cost too much.

"You looked so tired," she said. "The charcoal around your mouth and on your tongue from the hospital was still evident. Your eyes were sunken and lifeless. I remember how cold you were." I listened to her memories and, although painful, I knew retelling them was for both of our healing. Later on, she told me, "I could see in your eyes that something dramatic had changed in you, not just physically but also emotionally: you had let go. You looked stripped to the core, and you were letting people come alongside you and care for you." And they cared for me deeply—continuing to love on me by asking me how I was doing, continuing to ask me to go out and do things, and continuing to believe in me.

Now, in the car with Chris, I cried. He stopped the car in front of the restaurant, with the night sky beginning to move into a shade of gray. This was shame. Same naked shame from the hospital, the same shame I felt when I looked back and saw the people, the hearts and the relationships left as survivors in my eating disorder's path of destruction. Just because I was finally ready to move forward didn't mean everyone else was.

"I am sorry. I am sorry if I hurt your feelings," he said.

"No, don't be sorry. This is only a natural consequence of

what happened. These are the effects of it, and I have to face them. I can't run from them."

"We don't have to go in. We don't have to."

"Yes, we do. I am not going to let Ed win," I said, in between rubbing the tears from my face. "I am not going to numb out when I am uncomfortable. I am sorry for all the pain I caused you."

His hand to my head, he gently turned my face toward him and looked into me. "I love you, Lee. I hate the eating disorder. But I love you, Lee." He reached down and kissed my lips, telling me we were in this together. We went in, and I carefully talked with his family about my experience, being sensitive to their own very real hesitations about me: Will she do it again? Can we trust her? Is she really better?

As friends and family, and especially Chris, tossed these questions around, I would see them checking me in the extra glance at the table—to see if I really did finish that sandwich. Other times I saw it in the additional look, scanning my body as I walked away. I wanted to tell them—my friends and my family— and prove to them that I was getting better, to explain to them in detail all of the new experiences I was having and the foods I was able to eat. I wanted to tell them that I finally had grumbling again in my stomach when it wanted food. And then there was the return of my period, proving to me that my body could actually function again. *Did you know that?* I wanted to say. *Don't you believe me?* I wanted to yell.

Sometimes I would tell them, and other times I would just share it with Jan. She helped me understand what I could expect from my support people, especially those I had broken trust with by my suicide attempt. And, I would remind myself, I was not doing recovery for them. I was doing recovery for God. And for me. I needed to allow them to have their own experiences and their own judgments, and let those go. It did me no good to hold on or to try to prove myself. My role now was only to be true to the person, Lee.

I knew isolation led me to dark places, so I jumped into life. I called people when I was struggling, even if I was horribly ashamed. I went to therapy consistently, even when I didn't want to go. I ate foods I was afraid of. I slowly was able to resume exercising in moderation. Chris and I joined a couples' Bible study, and I joined the theater team at our church. I told everyone I was struggling with an eating disorder. I didn't want Ed to have a foothold anywhere. Even though I hated telling on myself when I was struggling, being vulnerable with strangers, and even having to check the "depression" box on the forms at the doctor's office, I knew all of it—being vulnerable and real— was better than wearing a mask. This helped me to live a more authentic life, and in return, my relationships were stronger and I was able to feel free about being myself.

trial

A *trial* is a formal examination of evidence by a judge, typically before a jury, in order to decide guilt in a case of criminal or civil proceedings. As a verb, it means to test something (especially a new product) to assess its suitability or performance.

Chris and I began seeing a pre-engagement counselor. Brad, who was still Chris's boss at Young Life, had recommended it. I was no dummy; I knew what was going on. Brad probably wanted to make sure Chris knew what he was getting into with me—and a professional counselor was just the one to offer that. Because, really, who marries a woman with a history like mine?

I was turning this over in my mind while decorating my new apartment. It was in a white building with large pillars—just a few blocks from Lake Harriet, where Chris and I had had our first date. I loved my new place, with my Laura Ashley bedspread on my new bed and the black futon Chris gave me for seating in the living room. As I shook the comforter out and placed it neatly on the mattress, I wondered, *Maybe it was Chris's dad's advice to put the "white elephant" under the microscope—to* prove, once and for all, that I was not good enough for his one and only son. I got it. The time in the restaurant went really well, but I got why he might be hesitant.

This counselor was nothing more than a smokescreen for what was really happening: Me. On trial.

I agreed to the therapy because I now was beginning to feel confident. My feet were firmly on the ground again, the weight slowly coming on, and the medication was taken daily, despite my fears. I was starting to believe in recovery, and I was sure this therapist would see that. I was also interested to find out what Chris's issues were, as I knew I couldn't be the only one with issues here.

We drove to a small town in Minnesota to meet this highly recommended counselor. The office was like an old ski lodge— dark wood, exposed beams and natural lighting shining through the windows. We entered the room boldly, hand in hand, smiling like a couple in love.

In his forties, Dr. Modene was reading, hunched over papers on his desk. He had small, dark eyes that looked sad.

Session one was a test with large packets of papers for us each to fill out. "You have thirty minutes," he instructed.

I hated tests, hated the way they put you in a box. And I really despised timed tests because I was so focused on winning and performing the fastest that I didn't take my time to do my best. I filled out the test anyway. Stupid test with little boxes to tell him who I was. Fine. Whatever. We both finished them, though I think I finished first, just for competition sake, and we turned them in. The therapist told us we would most likely need about six visits with him, which should be enough time to review the results of the tests.

Not bad. I could do six visits.

Well, six visits turned into eight. Then ten. Then I couldn't take it anymore. He scratched at me, this therapist. Those eyes were so cold, his tone so condescending to me. He was a very conservative Christian man who made it pretty clear about my role, the role of a woman. I was here to love and support my man, to obey him. I was supposed to fit in a box, and I didn't like it.

I sat in my chair, legs crossed, determination on my face. He, behind his big mahogany desk. Chris, to my right, comfortable and clueless to my brewing anger. He was caught up in the stirring of his own soul: Should he marry me? Should he not? What about all of my "red flags," as Dr. Modene called them. I imagined Modene's wife. Probably a large, blubbery woman with a big, thick turtleneck and headbands. Lots of brown leather headbands. I imagined this scenario in my head until I heard him say, "The scores on your test."

"Yes," we said.

He continued, "There are some red flags."

"Oh?" Chris said. I wondered if the phrase "red flags" was his exit door, to not fully commit to this relationship.

Dr. Modene's forehead wrinkled tight. He leaned a bit closer to us, like he was going to tell us a big secret. "You and Chris both scored a 10 on the spontaneity section. This concerns me."

I moved in my chair, changed my legs, my hands between the knees. I prepared for his words.

"If two people as spontaneous as you marry, there will be no one to put the brakes on in your marriage. No one to be the voice of reason. No one to put the foot down."

Chris turned his face to me, and I saw his eyes all bright and giggly. He smiled, and it touched me right in the center of my heart. He was speaking to me, and I knew what he was saying: *I love that about us.* Chris was on my side now.

Dr. Modene began to speak more firmly; obviously the two of us were not taking him seriously. He told us about these tests, the research done on couples and the chances of a couple with our scores working. "Well," he concluded, "it doesn't look good."

Chris responded lightly, "So my guess is what we did last night wouldn't look so good to you?"

"What do you mean?" he inquired.

"Lee and I were hanging out last night, looking for a little adventure, and we decided to go pool hopping."

"Pool what?" he asked, looking at me accusingly. Because, really, I was the crazy one there.

I am not sure if Chris was ignoring Dr. Modene's escalating concern or celebrating it. He continued, "Pool hopping. You know, where you sneak into an apartment complex or someone's backyard and jump in the pool with your clothes on? It is so fun!"

I was snickering.

Dr. Modene's face was all wide and shocked. He sat quietly behind his desk, unsure what to say. "Isn't that illegal?" he finally came up with.

Chris and I both threw our heads back and laughed, full-bellied laughter. Modene just stared at us in disbelief.

I loved the spontaneity in Chris. Loved it when I said, "Hey, let's do cartwheels in the Mall of America," and he said, "Sure." Extemporaneous singing, the funny accents, or the goofy ideas and stories we came up with. The two of us were constantly laughing and creating. Neither of us saying, "No, I don't think that is a good idea." We had many fun adventures together. Why would someone want to take that away?

Modene started his closing arguments. His stern advice was filled with words of caution about our too-similar personalities, about my highly dysfunctional past, and what the research showed. All I heard were words like Charlie Brown's teacher, mumbled *w*'s sounding like, "Wahh, wahh, wahh."

But after the laughter came tiny fissures of fear. Fear for both of us. I assumed Chris was afraid to hear a professional warning him. I, having very little trust in so-called professionals (except for my own therapist), was growing tired of this trial. Chris drove the car back to Minneapolis. Neither of us spoke, and I stared out the window into the stretch of highway. The thoughts began like a drumroll, slowly, then faster and faster: *He deserves some nice Christian girl with a clean past and a simple personality, someone without all that baggage. I am too much for him, too much.*

Chris said, "Modene must be sensitive to couples just starting out in marriage because he probably deals with so many couples that divorce. He is just trying to slow us down so we don't become one of those couples."

Who is in a hurry? I thought. Then I said, "I wasn't the one with the dream and the talk of marriage. I am just getting back on my feet, trying to figure out who the heck I am without an eating disorder, to figure out where I belong."

Then I became angry, "You are putting me through these tests because you are afraid."

I turned to him. He kept his head straight, hands gripped on the wheel. "What will everyone think if you marry someone who tried to take her own life? Someone who struggles to eat? With me, there are no guarantees. That has to be hard."

He didn't say anything—a common response when we argued. We rode the rest of the way home in silence.

I heard, very quietly, the voice. The mean voice of Ed, *Comfort and control.* I saw my reflection in the rearview mirror. The chubby cheeks. *Chubba, chubba, chubba,* I heard the younger me tease in the mirror. Ed said slyly, *I can help you get rid of those.*

Shut up, Ed, I thought. *I will not fall back into your trap. I can handle this. I will handle this.*

So I prayed. *God, guide me, please. Help us navigate these very choppy waters.*

Chris pulled the car to the curb, my white apartment building to the left, and moved the car in park. Still, he said nothing.

"I need some time to think," I said.

The leather seat rubbed under his large body as he twisted to me. His eyes looked hurt. They melted me.

Quietly, he said, "Lee, I am sorry. The therapy stuff, not what I expected either."

I was firm, a wall up. I didn't want to be hurt. I needed some time to think.

I took a deep breath and spoke my mind, a skill I had always had but masked so long by Ed. Not willing to quiet it anymore, I continued, "You need some time to think too, about what you really want. I don't want to be on trial like this anymore. This is me, and I am trying to learn to be who I am."

He looked down.

"You need to figure out if it is too scary for you to be with someone like me. You obviously aren't sure yet, since it seems like you have to get everyone's stamp of approval. I am not going to be put through this anymore. I need time to think."

"Are you okay?" he asked, and gently touched my hand. The same hand in the same car that dark October day. But the same woman wasn't sitting in that seat. I was no longer fragile and unsure, no longer tangled in the darkness of depression and the slyness of Ed. I had a voice, my voice, and I was learning to use it. And it felt good.

"Yes, I am okay." I believed myself. *I am okay.* I said, maybe out loud or maybe in my head, *I am okay—just the way I am.* I reached over and kissed him on the cheek. His smell was tantalizing and pulled me to want to soothe this all over, to make it better. But I didn't. I could now sit with uncomfortable feelings, so I exited the car and slowly shut the door before I walked to my apartment.

I loved him, I knew. I knew it like I knew when I woke in the morning that the sun was going to rise. Or when I went to bed at night, I knew that there were stars in the sky somewhere. I knew I loved him like that knowing. But I also knew, as I learned to have a voice, that I could only let it go so far. It wasn't my job to prove to him that I would be well. I didn't know if that was the truth, me being well. It was a risk *he* had to take, and I couldn't do it for him.

Recognizing the things over which I was powerless had taught me I couldn't control this situation. But now as I entered the building, my shoulders tightened, my hands gripped, and there was me, all mad—hot anger in my joints and in my head, mixing me up and telling me to use old coping skills.

I had been using affirmations as fuel to fight Ed, but now, twisted in my head, I heard, *You won't ever be well.* The voice I was trying to push away, badgered.

I was on the spinning ride again. Nothing making sense.

I walked up the stairs to my apartment, opened the large, oversized door and then slammed it shut. I plodded into the kitchen and saw a large, colorful sign in reds and yellows and blues. Taped to the cabinets it screamed at me: HALT!

Are you hungry, angry, lonely, tired?

"I am angry!" I said back to it. My face mean and scrunched up. My hands on my hips. "Really mad!"

Underneath my foot I could feel the piece of linoleum that tore when I moved my table in. I hated that rip in the floor. I looked down and kicked it. *Why doesn't someone fix that?* Then I bent down and tugged at it. It pulled up easy.

I ripped another piece that started to tear from the first piece. Pulled and then tossed hard. Small pieces of black-and-white linoleum, thrown at the wall, at the cabinets and into the living room—one after the other. The anger in my hands felt beneath the tiles. I smelled the rough, pungent glue, and I saw the old dirt in the sticky mess holding it all together. It was grimy, and my knees were smothered in white dust from the friction of the pulling.

Ed pulled at me like I pulled at the linoleum. I resisted. I didn't give in. And God pulled harder. The conversations replayed over and over in my mind, and I saw Chris's sweet face, those eyes warming me.

But I also saw his hesitation.

And then I remembered the night in the restaurant, fighting Ed, the two of us—together.

I moved to the edge of the kitchen. The tiles were stronger there. My arms were losing strength, but I kept ripping and pulling. I was replaying the scene when we walked into that restaurant, hand in hand. A team. The two of us, talking about the elephant in the room, telling the story of the hospital—even if others were uncomfortable. The two of us, fighting together against Ed.

I didn't feel like we were a team now. I pulled up another piece, and it sliced my hand. "Ouch!" I screamed.

I paused. It hurt. It actually hurt. I was feeling and felt the real pain of a cut—instead of cutting to inflict pain. I knew I was moving forward and changing. I was kicking Ed in the dust. To the curb. I got off my knees and went into the bathroom when I heard the phone ring. I didn't answer. The answering machine did and I heard his deep, tender voice.

"Hey, I just wanted to see if you are okay. If you want to talk, call me later." He paused, "Okay?"

I heard it crack. The voice.

I wanted to call him back, but I didn't. Space would help. He needed space. It was not my job to fix him. Not his job to fix me.

After a few hours, the adrenaline started to dissipate and my body and thoughts began to settle down. I remembered Jan telling me, "Emotions are like a wave. They come and go, but they can't stay one way forever. Just ride the wave."

I rode it—without the eating disorder. It felt really nice. I smiled. Then my stomach mumbled. It was hungry, the cues were back, and I went into the kitchen and ate.

I was going to be okay—with or without Chris. I was going to be okay. I looked down at the huge mess in the kitchen. Ripped up tiles everywhere, with dust and yellow glue, sticky and dry. I left it. The mess on the floor was better than me messing up my body.

Lying in bed I stared into the ceiling and cried, the wave hitting me again. What if it was over? I would have to move forward without him. Better he left now than when he couldn't handle it anymore.

The left side of my chest began to ache. I put my hand on my chest. It wasn't the eating-disorder chest pain. It was the pain of a broken relationship. I would not run from it. *I will feel it. I will live,* I said to myself, and to God, as I fell into sleep.

the church with
the red door

The stories we tell ourselves: I had lots of them. Stories about how selfish I was. Stories that told me I was a morning person. Stories given to me by others, about how bad I was. Stories telling me I was energetic. Stories I told myself about my future as a Broadway star.

My story wasn't going to include a husband or a family. I saw the mess that created and had no interest. I also didn't plan on having my story weave in an eating disorder or a suicide attempt.

"If we stay in the story we tell ourselves, we can miss the story God has for us," the pastor at church said. I wanted to be in control of my story so no one could hurt me again. God wanted to be in control of my story so he could show me his unending love for his creation, for me. At the crossroad of my story and God's story, the question arose, Which way do I go? How do I know which way to go?

A sliver of white sunlight cast a line on the wall in my small room. The morning held newness and a fresh start. *White as snow,* I thought of God and his words about his mercies being new every morning. I soaked the sunlight in while lying in my bed, soaked it in with my breath. A cool breeze sifted through my open window. It was the morning before Easter, the day before the resurrection, when it would all make sense.

Rebirth.

Flowers were opening their arms, and air was fresh with warm touches of spring. The sun was beginning to melt the enormous piles of dirty snow left in the corners of parking lots, and the people, lots of people, beginning to emerge outside again. I thought of the year ahead—whatever it might bring—how it had to be better than the last. As only a year ago, I was lying in a hospital bed.

I got up slowly out of my bed, the cold wood hard against my bare toes. A sinking swept over me. A drop in my heart when I recalled the evening before. I knew my story didn't include a husband, so it made sense to let it go.

Walking into my kitchen, having forgotten, my eyes opened wide. *Wow, I made quite a mess.*

Tiles, and scraps of tiles, were strewn everywhere, so I had to maneuver my way through the kitchen. I walked out of the destruction to the futon Chris lent me. I sat, hands clasped, eyes closed in prayer. I told God about the anger, my frustrations with Chris and his "test," my temptation to go back to Ed, my fear of the future and, eventually, my thankfulness for being alive—even if it was confusing, even if it was scary.

I remembered a verse I had recently memorized, and I spoke it out loud: "Let the morning bring me word of your unfailing love, for I have put my trust in you. Show me the way I should go, for to you I entrust my life" (Psalm 143:8).

My story was changing. Chris had believed a dream, but I

had questioned this belief. I continued my resolve to do the work, fighting Ed, and believe in a future, even if that future was hard. I had to. Ed was not an option.

Yet the love that warmed my heart and created sweat in my palms wanted to call him, to tell him what I was thinking and how I was feeling. He, the one I always told. I resisted. I moved on with my day. Breakfast. Got dressed. Planned for a walk. Chose life.

Only minimal exercise allowed still, with my fragile heart recovering. My emotions made that first meal difficult. Ed telling me not to eat when I was all mixed up. I said out loud: *Not an option. You are not an option.* I ate my breakfast. *One choice toward life for the day,* I thought. While rinsing my dishes in the sink, I heard the phone ring and let the answering machine get it.

"Lee, Lee, are you there? Please pick up. I really need to talk to you."

I ran to it.

"Hi," I said coldly, for protection.

He didn't cue into my lack of emotion: "I have to come over. Please. Can I come over?"

Warm, heated heart. "Okay fine, but I am going down to the lake in twenty minutes, so you better come over now," I said.

My mind reminded me that I had decided to end our relationship last night. My heart was pulling me back to him. I tried to reason with it, telling it to behave.

He was at my door within minutes. I opened it, and his tall presence stood in my doorway. I softened, tummy fluttering. I laughed at his hair sticking out like a chicken. "Nice hair," I say.

He smiles, "Nice kitchen floor."

He was wearing the same green nylon pants, green jacket and running shoes he had been wearing on the day we met. So much between that time. The day we met. Now.

The space between us was erased by his tight hug.

I pulled away. Turned around and walked into my bedroom. On the edge of the bed, I sat rigid. I loved him. I knew I did. But I was afraid of his uneasiness regarding me.

He sat on the floor, his legs stretched long. Looking up, he said, "Lee, I am sorry. I am sorry for putting you through all of this—sorry for making you feel tested."

Tiny tears grew in my eyes.

"I am sorry for not believing in you."

I kept my wall up, yet my heart leaped. "Chris, I just can't do this anymore. I can't be in this relationship if you can't accept me as me."

The story, I was learning to accept me as me. I was beginning to have a voice, and part of that voice was not allowing others to contribute to any more of my disbelief in the hope of a future. I couldn't handle others' doubt because I had enough of my own.

"This is who I am. The full package. Either you love it or leave it. I am doing the best I can to fight Ed and my old habits, and this person," I pointed at my heart, "this is the person you fell in love with."

■   ■   ■

White dress, simple and feminine. My hair pulled up with only a few spiral curls hanging down, and the thin, white veil in front of my face: Our wedding day. He had asked me spontaneously on the same day he came to my apartment with the chicken hair. Without hesitation, I said, "YES!"

Not even a year after my suicide attempt. I knew the whispers of those who had been on the journey with me, those who stood in that hospital, standing over my frail body near death. They had reason to be concerned and afraid; I would have been if I were them. But I wasn't. I knew in every part of me that I was making the right decision.

What did the future hold? I had no idea. But I knew life was meant to be lived, and for me, living meant making my own decisions that I felt God was leading me to make. And now, to live my life with the man I loved. He had changed too, reading books on eating disorders and going to therapy sessions with Jan. He began to understand how to help me as well.

Dad walked slowly up next to me and linked his arm in mine. He was stunning and handsome in his black-and-white tuxedo. I began to feel my knees shake and my heart ache. I loved Dad so much. He turned his face to me and quietly whispered, "I love you, LeeWolfe. I am so proud of you."

How, I wondered, could he be proud of a daughter who put him through hell and back in the last year? Then, after thousands of dollars in treatment, I asked for him to pay for a wedding. But really, after I finally let go of striving for approval from him, it finally came: on my wedding day.

"I am so proud of you."

I savored those words and agreed. I was proud of me too, and so thankful for him affirming me.

"I love you, Daddy," I said, my eyes filled with tears. "Thank you for all of your support."

Every single cell in me felt as if I was living in a different body than the one I had been living in for the past few years. I felt new. I felt at peace.

I think now of the verse in Revelation, "And the one sitting on the throne said, 'Look, I am making everything new!' And then he said to me, 'Write this down, for what I tell you is trustworthy and true'" (21:5 NLT).

Dad and I walked slowly down the red carpet guiding our

path, and I smiled wide while gazing at the man standing ahead waiting. Chris, with his tan face and dark black hair, his shoulders broad and strong. Chris, despite his fears and concerns, was willing to take the risk. With me.

"I want to be with you forever; we can get through whatever comes our way," he would repeat.

There were no guarantees for us; it could be a difficult life.

But Chris was able to love me, not the eating disorder. He was able to see me without the eating disorder and to continue loving that part of me. "I love you. I hate Ed," he would say. And soon, I began to love me and hate Ed with him. The two of us on the battle lines, fighting to keep Ed away.

Classical music played loudly, echoing in the deep crevices of the beautiful, old church. Stained glass, beautiful woodwork, a fiery red door. We didn't attend this church, but I felt it fit us perfectly. At the altar stood my two attendants: Wendy, blond and angelic-looking, had a heart of gold and her support was unending. She is still the first to send me an encouraging note, usually telling me, "I am your biggest fan." My sister, who at this time was only beginning to become a close friend, was my other attendant. While my eating disorder had been too difficult for her to talk about, our relationship was blooming into a deep friendship. Two of Chris's biggest supporters stood on his side: his roommate Matt and his dad. Chris's dad had become more than willing to learn about eating disorders in order to understand them. He had come a long way since that day in October.

When Dad gave me to Chris, Chris lifted the veil and, leaning down to look at me, said, "You are beautiful."

And you know what? I felt beautiful.

My weight was almost to the goal weight set by my dietitian, my body now functioning like a woman. And with a steady diet of food, my emotions were less chaotic. I felt whole. And I had a new rule in my life: Never skip a meal—no matter what. That is how I protected myself. Despite what others are doing, even to this day, I eat.

Our hands tightly intertwined, we turned to the pastor, Perry Hunter, the regional director for Young Life and a special friend. A hot, sweltering day in July, there was no air conditioning in the church, and sweat was pouring off Perry. Caught up in it all, I barely noticed the heat, and during the ceremony, I think I whispered "thank you, God" a thousand times.

The story was changing, and I let it change. I wanted it to change.

And then an angelic voice filled the chapel as a friend sang "Amazing Grace."

How sweet the sound.

She beautifully filled the sanctuary with her strong, tender voice.

That saved a wretch like me.

The words to my choice of a song.

I once was lost. But now am found. Was blind but now I see.

Chris and I looked into each other's eyes, both of us crying. Tears of joy. Tears of gratitude to feel part of a story bigger than ourselves, something so powerful, called Amazing Grace.

How did I go from a suicide attempt to walking down the aisle with the man of my dreams? It was rocky but wonderful. While living with the eating disorder, I existed in a world of black and white, of all or nothings. Without the eating disorder guiding my way, my new way of life was gray and unclear. My emotions, when set free and no longer confined by Ed's instructions, were all over the place. My job was to trust. Trust that God would do his part as long as I did mine.

As Perry announced, "We are happy to welcome Mr. and Mrs. Christopher Blum," the crowd clapped and cheered, and Chris and I skipped like children down the aisle while hooting and hollering. On my side of the church, sat all my parents. Joe was there, as I honored him for being such a good friend in my life. Mom brought her new boyfriend, and Dad brought his girl-friend, Debbie, whom he eventually married. Over the years, she had become one of the greatest gifts in my family, a woman with a kind heart, and one of my biggest cheerleaders. My surrogate parents, Dave and Judy Carver, were there at the most crucial time in my life, and they read Scripture at the service.

Also there was Jan, my therapist, who sat alongside my amazing and supportive friends. Friends from Young Life and friends from church. Friends that knew me in all my messiness and loved me anyway. All of them, the whole community, witnessing and experiencing God's amazing work, that day there to share in the glory.

The wedding was beautiful, but it was also something else. It was healing, healing for the pack of people who had been through the dark places with me. All of us together in one room, celebrating. Yes, they were celebrating a union between two people. But I think they were also celebrating life.

Life redeemed.

Life that was almost stolen away. A covenant redeemed, and it had not even been a full year.

They were witness to it all, and truly, it was by amazing grace. "For it is by grace you have been saved, through faith—and this is not from yourselves, it is the gift of God—not by works, so that no one can boast" (Ephesians 2:8-9).

two lines

Recovery is like a roller coaster: ups and downs, tight turns, whips of the head. The first of year of marriage, while rebuilding my life was, let's just say, less than ideal.

A wild roller coaster ride.

I wouldn't allow myself to skip meals, so I had to face the reality of emotions as well as a new body. Without the eating disorder I became like a frantic animal, looking for anything to cling to. I trusted and clung to God. Most of my journals from this time are no longer filled with wallowing about life but, rather, rich theological study. Yet in moments of discontent and fear, whispers of Ed would sneak in and catch me off guard.

It happened right before our first wedding anniversary. In truth, until recently, I had forgotten about this but Chris hadn't.

We were settled into my apartment, now *our* place. His over-sized speakers, dart board and plant were about the extent of his decorating additions. He fixed the floors I had destroyed with nice, shiny tile. And I was enrolled in two classes at the University of Minnesota to finally finish my degree, since I'd had to drop out of the other classes when I went into treatment. Kansas University let my credits transfer, and I eventually received my diploma. I had a job at Bruegger's Bagels and had no idea what I would do for a job in the future.

Jan was adamant that I take the changes slow. She would constantly remind me, "You are used to a pattern of constant change: changing schools, changing your body, changing jobs, even changing states. You need to be still and be patient."

This "staying" left me with an enormous amount of anxiety. Chris was often gone at night or out of town with his Young Life job. On this particular night, I found myself in the bathroom. Razor in hand. Cutting myself on my wrist for punishment. I wasn't suicidal, but I was using an old coping mechanism to relieve pain. I have no memory of what triggered this, so it is hard to explain. Why, when my life was going so well and I was finally using my voice, would I harm myself? Because sometimes, somewhere deep inside, I would still feel like I didn't deserve the good. *It shouldn't be so good. Why should life be so good? Better mess it up before something else does.* I went to bed that night, alone and ashamed.

Had I relapsed? Had I fallen off the wagon?

I kept it a secret, and I knew I was playing with fire. Because Ed loves secrets.

The secret lasted only a day, until I went into Jan's office and told her about it. She insisted I tell Chris. When I did, he was crushed and angry. Today, when he tells the story, he says it was almost as bad for him as it was the day I attempted suicide. He stood in the shower the evening after I confessed and bawled like a baby, crying out to God, deep in fear: *Is this the life we will be living?* Would it be one where he couldn't leave his wife alone, couldn't trust her not to harm herself?

No.

That was the last time I ever cut myself. We went to see Jan, came up with a plan and began to recover from the incident together. For a year or two, we had a razor-free house unless I asked Chris to check one out for me to use. Without the eating disorder and without cutting, I was left to feel. And being the passionate and sensitive person I am, I feel hard and deep. I had to relearn how to feel and how to let the feelings be what they are. It took time, but it happened.

■   ■   ■

"Jesus looked at them intently and said, 'Humanly speaking, it is impossible. But with God everything is possible'" (Matthew 19:26 NLT).

That December, winter had already made herself at home, bringing in massive amounts of snow. In our bedroom in our beautiful new home in St. Paul, Chris sat on the cream-colored duvet in his usual attire, workout pants and a sweatshirt. "I won't believe it until I hear it from a doctor," he said.

Laughing at his ridiculousness, I said, "I will get it and show it to you!"

I was wearing a business suit, my "power suit," as Chris called it. I had a fantastic job as a conference planner, traveling all over the United States, staying in fancy hotels and putting on events. My job was to obsess over all the particulars and organize every detail. The perfectionism that was used for my eating disorder was now a gift when used for my job, instead of harming myself. I had a recovery toolbox, and I was frequently using all of the tools—calling friends for support, going to therapy, taking care of myself and, most of all, feeling my emotions. On this day, my body, wearing a navy blue suit and a silky T-shirt, was in the maintenance stage of recovery, and my weight had been stable for the past four-and-a-half years. The eating disorder was now like a bad ex-boyfriend, locked deep in the dungeon of my soul. The only person who was able to set him free was me. But I had no interest in going back.

Life had brought more life—life full with relationships and love and sorrow and joy. Of course I was still learning how to live with my voice, to have healthy relationships, to set boundaries. But when the eating disorder had initially presented itself, it snowballed out of control. When I started making choices toward life, the snowball of recovery consumed me in the same fashion. I was determined not to return to it.

And what happened on this day sealed the deal for me.

I walked down the long, old hallway to our tiny bathroom. I picked up the stick sitting on the counter and rushed back to our bedroom to show him. Tingly inside, it felt unreal, like we were witnessing a miracle. And, really, we were. I looked down at the stick just to be sure: two blue lines. I was pregnant.

"See!" I said holding the stick in the air and shaking it at him. "Two lines. There are really two lines!"

"Really? Let me see that thing!"

Shocked. This body that had been beaten and bruised by Ed, this body forever with scars, was able to hold a life.

We cried.

"We are pregnant! We are pregnant! A baby! I can't believe we are having a baby!" we squealed, jumping up and down.

A child. A gift. A miracle. We were ecstatic and awed.

For some people who struggle with eating disorders, pregnancy can be quite triggering. For me, it was the final piece of letting my eating disorder go. A baby was growing in me, and I was learning to have a relationship with my body unlike one I had ever had. I was fully alive and had life inside of me.

I learned to allow my body to do what it needed to, not to

push it too hard but to be gentle. Eating became intuitive, and it was around this time when I was finally able to relinquish following a rigid meal plan. My body and I became friends. I began to trust it and listen to it. And, often during this time, it would tell me it wanted donuts. I gave it donuts whenever it wanted—even on church Sundays.

26

shedding

"Amazing grace, how sweet the sound." Rich, deep, soulful sounds from the David Crowder Band sang on the radio alarm clock. It is early. I slam my hand down on the white button to make it stop. The morning is dark, calling me back to sleep, away from the coming day. I had planned to get up early. I decide I am too tired. A part of recovery is listening to my body when it says *rest*. I listen. Chris, and his entourage of six pillows around his body, lies oblivious to the noise. I pull my soft down comforter up under my chin, hoping for a few more minutes of slumber.

"Mom? Mom?" A different alarm clock now wakes me, a human alarm. "Mom? Mom?" a soft voice next to our bed repeats until I open my heavy eyes to my seven-year-old, Matthew. With his sandy blond hair a crumpled mess on top of his head and one very large, adult tooth sprouting in the spaces where his baby teeth were, my firstborn—still my baby, still my miracle—is growing so quickly.

"Can I have some cold milk?" he says groggily, his slit-like eyes in between half asleep and half awake.

"In a minute," I whisper to him as I lift down my comforter, an invitation for snuggle time. He climbs into our bed, slipping into the small space next to me.

"Good morning" I say, sliding my right arm underneath his head and embracing him close to me.

I remind myself to remember this, to capture it. Moments like this, thousands of them come with recovery, moments of love and tenderness. This gift of life, in my arms, is growing up so quickly I can barely keep up.

Had I died that day I would have missed this.

I remember every day. Every day, I look in their eyes. I remember and I know: I would have missed this.

In moments like these, I hear a small voice within. It is my own voice, now gentle and kind. It gained courage to speak in recovery. Only when I first stopped listening to Ed and the mean voices Ed brought with him, did I begin to hear my own voice. My voice now helps me live, fully alive, embracing life in all its complexities. And my voice also now comforts that little girl who spent so many years crying in her bedroom, striving to be better, longing for approval. This voice, my voice, the voice God gave me, tells me, *You are enough. Just as you are.*

I wrap my arm tighter around Matthew and press my face gently against the back of his little head, inhaling the smell of his grape-shampooed hair. His breathing slow, in and out, while he glides into sleep. I'm sandwiched between Chris and Matthew, their alternate breathing creating a musical tune. A powerful thought pulses through my veins.

Gratefulness.

From my fingertips to my toes, gratefulness fills every pore— in my arms, my legs, up to the top of my head. I feel this often, this gratefulness. Because I have been in the dark pit of what felt like hell. And I *never* want to be in it again. But when you have been in that dark space, the sunshine and the joy is even more powerful. I know how horrible life can be, which makes the sweet moments even sweeter, and in these moments, I want to (and often do) fall on my knees. Laying my head in the lap of God, sitting casually in a rocking chair with his arms out wide, I cry out: *Thank you. Thank you.*

Later in the kitchen, I go straight to Mr. Coffee for my morning cup. Impatiently, I stand waiting for the coffee to brew when, behind me, I hear the patter of little feet on the tile floor. A small boy-voice behind me bursts out, "Boo!" I turn around and pretend to be scared. My second son, Michael, runs and hides beneath his red-and-blue Clifford sleeping bag in a heap on our couch. His little head with bright blond hair peeks out, he looks up at me and again yells, "Boo!"

Michael is my morning sunshine.

A five-year-old, overflowing with energy and joy. I walk quickly to him and reach under the polyester bag to tickle his warm body. Giggles under the blanket. Then, he dramatically throws his sleeping bag off his slight body, his bright blue eyes wide with wonder, "Good morning! What are we having for breakfast?"

I sit next to him and pull him close. Michael, or my mini-me, as I like to call him, is full of energy and spirit, which can often be overwhelming. When I look at his flaxen hair and his intense, blue eyes filled with eagerness, I am reminded of myself: of a spirit so bursting with excitement and energy that it prompted Mom and Dad to yell, their faces red with frustration at their rambunctious child, "Slow down. You think too much. Stop going so fast!"

I don't blame them now. Maturity, recovery and years of therapy helped me rebuild my relationship with my own parents. They did the best they could with what they had. I was, as I am learning with Michael, not the easiest kid to parent. "Spirited children" is what they call them now, and they can be a handful. So, with Michael, I am careful not to crush his collection of energy and his deep sensitivity with words like "too much." I am hoping to teach him that his personality, so frighteningly like mine, is a gift to be used wisely.

Mornings are chaotic when I haven't had my morning time— time with God or alone on a short run at the lake. But lately I have chosen to sleep longer, trying to listen to my body and its cries for more sleep or more rest—letting go of the urges to "do."

I hear gurgling from Mr. Coffee, and I jump to retrieve my morning joe. The cold, plastic mug is tightly secured by my left hand when I lower my eyes, seeing the three small scars, boldly imprinted on my left wrist. I wonder when the boys will notice, when they will ask, what will I say about these lines that are forever on my arm?

I don't know. All I know is today. Today is good. Chris enters the kitchen with a sleepy two-and-a-half-year-old Tommy on his hip, his head lying on Chris's shoulder. I walk over and kiss Tommy's sweet little face, with those long eyelashes, sewn on by angels, resting on his cheeks.

My life. My family.

Later, after our messy breakfast, I stand for a moment. The kitchen dishes piled in the sink and scattered crumbs on the floor, I am drawn to the beautiful maple tree that stands proudly outside the window. Almost prematurely, today the tree is shedding its crisp, auburn leaves. In twos and threes, I watch their descent from the thin branches of the tree, dancing down to the ground. In only a few days, all of the beautiful, ginger foliage will abandon the tree, leaving it bare and naked.

The shedding leaves, the crisp air and the squirrels gathering in to prepare for hibernation still remind me of that dark autumn day. Still remind me of how bleak life felt. How trapped and how close to death I was. Like it was yesterday yet so long ago, the girl seems like a different person, someone I no longer know.

Twelve years earlier, when autumn cold represented death and darkness, and when naked trees left me feeling alone and afraid, I now see the leaves dancing toward their roots through a new lens, reinforcing something much different. This lens is clear and sharp. It shows thankfulness, joy, growth. And I, along with the trees, shed the layers. The layers of protection surrounding my soul are falling off. Pieces land softly in the air as I learn to trust, learn not to run—as I learn to let go of the me I thought I was supposed to be to become the me God wants me to be.

"When I am growing toward the me I want to be, I am being freed from the me I pretend to be."

The change continues because, although food is not an issue now, the walls that were built during the time of my eating disorder have taken years to come down. But God knows what he is doing. And I know he is with me always. He always was, really. "'For I know the plans I have for you,' says the LORD. 'They are plans for good and not for disaster, to give you a future and a hope'" (Jeremiah 29:11 NLT).

peace

Peace. It does not mean to be in a place
where there is no noise or trouble or hard work.
It means to be in the midst of those things
and still be calm in your heart.

UNKNOWN

"Do you miss it?"

She stands behind the nurse's station where I am sitting. She is beautiful with smooth skin, full lips and perfectly almond-shaped eyes. She hates herself. It breaks my heart to see her hating. We who work with her see her without her eating disorder and see what is God's beautiful, amazing creation. I can't force her to see what I see. I only pray and walk alongside her, hoping someday she will see. I work at a hospital for eating disorders. I like to think of myself as a wounded healer, hoping to share hope with those who have lost it.

Quietly, she asks again, "Do you miss the eating disorder?"

"No," I say, looking deep into her hurting eyes. "No. Never."

She acts shocked, her eyes big. For her, the eating disorder is her best friend, her identity. She can't imagine life without it.

I was her. I couldn't imagine life without Ed.

"You have to believe God has something more for you than this. You have to believe it, and then do what you need to do, what we are telling you to do. You have to open the toolbox and use the tools."

"I don't know if I believe it," she says.

"That is why it is called *faith*," I remind her, even though I know recovery isn't as simple as one Bible verse or one prayer.

This book is just one story. There are millions out there with stories like mine but different, because recovery is not the same for anyone. This story is just how it was for me. I don't expect everyone else's to be the same.

But there are some key things that need to happen for someone to recover from an eating disorder, and I speak here from my own experience, as well as from working day to day with patients on the front lines of the battle with Ed. My hope and prayer is that these messages came through in this story because it is crucial to have these things in place for recovery to take hold. I like to call them, "Lee's Seven Keys":

1. Powerlessness: admit you are powerless over the eating disorder, and give the control to God—not halfway but 100 percent. So no keeping Ed in your back pocket for "just in case."

2. A good therapist: you will need a therapist that you will be open and honest with, *and* who has experience treating eating disorders.

3. A registered dietitian—not just a nutritionist but an R.D.—

and possibly a psychiatrist: both are crucial to help in recovery. I needed to see my dietitian until I was about two years into recovery, when I was able to start eating intuitively. I needed her support and accountability until I finally felt secure doing it on my own.

4. A support group or therapy group: this group isn't meant to be a social group but a place where you can say, "I am struggling," and have others hold you accountable.

5. Soul "food": by this I mean a Bible study group, people you can learn, grow and do life with. I have been in a Bible study with the same group of women for over ten years. It feeds my soul, builds deep relationships and helps me grow closer to God. It is also a form of accountability because the people really know me and can hold me accountable when I need it. A good church community can also be your soul food.

6. Body "food": taking care of your body is just as important as taking care of your soul. Find a place that is balanced and not too extreme where you can work out. Holy yoga is a great option.

7. Volunteering: I was blessed that Young Life still let me volunteer, and by helping others, I was able to see the world as a bigger place and get out of my head for a while. Volunteering helped me have a sense of purpose.

These are the things that were crucial to my recovery. As of this writing, it has been seventeen years since I almost lost my life. I consider myself recovered. I believe in recovery and believe it is possible for everyone.

Could I relapse? Sure. Do I want to? No. Do I miss it? NO! Do I miss the constant obsessing, the numbness, the inability to feel, the crazy thoughts, the body obsession, the counting of calories and the mind-numbing madness of Ed? Never. Not ever do I miss it.

I want to live.

I want to be alive *and* feel.

Because I know that life on the other side of an eating disorder is colorful, unorganized, messy and exquisitely beautiful. Life in the last seventeen years has been full: full of immense joy with the births of my children, full of deep sadness at two miscarriages, full of tremendous growth as I developed into womanhood, full of struggles in marriage and struggles in career, and also full of loads and loads of fun.

Life.

All of it.

The good *and* the bad.

Without Ed.

Full.

Why would I want to go back to the dark pit with Ed? I do not believe eating disorders are choices. But recovery is. It is a choice that has to be made one step at a time, one day at a time, one bite at a time.

Knowing myself now, I know I have the tendency to go to extremes with anything. I can easily get obsessed if I am not careful; it is in my genetic makeup. There have been only about three times in the last sixteen years where I felt Ed enticing me. These were during difficult times when I would hear a small whisper say, *Don't eat.* I remember them exactly, Ed telling me it was too much, too much pain, to come numb out. Those few times, I had to do it anyway. I had to do the work in spite of my emotions—right away. I walked into my kitchen, sobbing my eyes out, and ate my lunch anyway. No way was I going to let Ed get a foothold. Ever.

I protect my recovery.

And what about my parents? I hope the message is clear that

my parents didn't cause my eating disorder. In hindsight it might have helped if there was more validation for my personality or a wider repertoire of coping skills. However, although there was plenty of modeling in my family that I naturally copied, even if things had been different, I might still have ended up in the same place. Either way, I don't blame anyone anymore. My relationship with my family is strong now. The road to get here with them was a crazy, bumpy one, and I never imagined we could have such harmonious relationships now with all we went through then. Though our relationships took years to rebuild, I am so thankful for my family. What they put up with and what they had to go through, and the entire time, they continued to say, "We support you. We believe you can do this." Sure, there were other messages that weren't positive along the way, but my ability to see through the fog was skewed at that point.

My recovery story was not one of a straight line or one with an overnight rebirth, but it was a journey, a struggle. My story is one of a woman who lost her voice and found it again. It is a story about freedom, redemption and God's amazing, amazing grace. And with the amazing grace came the need for forgiveness, forgiveness so I could let go of all those arrows carrying negative messages. So I could smash those tapes and start playing new ones. God forgave me, and I needed to forgive others. Recovery isn't about praying a prayer and you get healed. In my story, there was a prayer for healing, but then I had to get in the game. I had to do the work—with God's help. Won't you also allow God to repair and restore you? I promise you. It is worth it.

"Come to me all who are weary and burdened, and I will give you rest" (Matthew 11:28).

AMEN.

acknowledgments

They believed in this story, and for that, I am so grateful to Elaina Whittenhall and Cindy Bunch at InterVarsity Press, who took a risk on a first-time author. My editor, Cindy Bunch, not only believed in the core of this story but was gentle and wise as she urged me to refine and cut the story down. I could not have worked with a better editor. And thank you to the amazing team at InterVarsity Press for all of their enthusiasm for this book.

Furthermore, everyone should have a friend like Wendy, who encouraged, supported, and read every single revision of this book—thank you, dear friend. To all my friends who held me through the writing process and continued, year after year, to believe in this book when I couldn't: Dena, Rhonda, Cameon and Jeff Carver, J. Johnson, Julie Greene and Kelly Robert. Thank you to my women's Bible study for the years of prayers, and thank you to Heather Larson for all of the therapy runs, prayers and lifelong friendship.

Thanks, too, to my amazing writing group, Prinna, Shannon and Kristin, for all the continued encouragement, and to the Loft Literary Center for the fantastic classes. Thank you to Jen Abbas and Constance Rhodes as well—for all of your help when I decided to actually write this book. Thank you, Katie Hopper, for all of your wise input on the format of this book. Thank you, Tove, for teaching me how to be in my body and to appreciate and love it. Tove, you are a gift.

A deep thank you also goes to my sweet sister, Kristin, for all of her support throughout this process, and to my brother, Corky, and his wife, Deb, for housing a very sick me and being so supportive during such a terrible time in my journey. To Mom, Dad and Debbie, thank you for continuing to support me and believe in me when I couldn't.

Thank you, Lori, for your friendship at Menninger—and to this day. I am forever grateful for Dave and Judy Carver for showing me authentic grace and love. To Jan Zahner, my wonderful, amazing therapist for believing in me when I couldn't.

And to the four amazing boys in my life—my husband, Chris, and my three sons—every day I look in your eyes and think *I would have missed this* had I died that day. Thank you for all of the times you believed in and supported me, for all the hours you let me shut myself in my office, for all the hugs and tears that you wiped away from my face after each book rejection or when I just couldn't do it anymore. You four are my everything, and I love you more than words could ever express.

notes

p. 95   "humbly asked him to remove our shortcomings": Friends in Recovery, *The Twelve Steps for Christians*, rev. ed. (Scotts Valley, CA: RPI Publishing, 1994).

p. 167   to assess its suitability or performance: This definition is loosely taken from Wikipedia, s.v. "trial," https://en.wikipedia.org/wiki/Trial, accessed September 2011.

p. 182   "Was blind but now I see": John Newton, "Amazing Grace," public domain.

p. 193   "freed from the me I pretend to be": John Ortberg, *The Me I Want to Be* (Grand Rapids: Zondervan, 2010), p. 24.

p. 197   it is in my genetic makeup: Michael J. Devlin, Joel Jahraus and Ilyse Dobrow Di Marco, *The American Psychiatric Publishing Textbook of Psychosomatic Medicine* (Arlington, VA: American Psychiatric Publishing), p. 12. "Many such trait factors (such as perfectionism, impulsivity, negative affect, and low self-esteem) may be largely genetically determined, and the genetics of eating disorders is a rapidly developing area of interest."

About the Author

Lee Wolfe Blum lives in Edina, Minnesota, with her husband and three boys. Her speaking includes

- Professional conferences on eating disorders
- Training staff who are working with patients who struggle with both an eating disorder and chemical dependency
- Health education conferences training health and PE teachers on eating disorders, body image and nutrition
- Schools (private and public) on the topics of nutrition, body image and eating disorders
- Women's groups, MOPS groups and church groups on
  - Women and body image (with the focus on moms)
  - Anxiety
  - Parenting your children to love their bodies
  - Debunking mental illness
- Her personal story
- Training youth pastors on mental illness, cutting, eating disorders and addictions
- Coteaching with her husband on what to do when your spouse has an eating disorder
- Recovery workshops at halfway houses

  You can contact Lee and learn more at leewolfeblum.com.

A reader's group guide is available at ivpress.com
and recovery resources are available
at leewolfeblum.com.

IVP *Crescendo*
COURAGE. CONFIDENCE. CALLING.

Some voices challenge us. Others support or encourage us. Voices can move us to change our minds, draw close to God, discover a new spiritual gift. The voices of others are shaping who we are.

The voices behind IVP Crescendo join together to draw us into God's story. We'll discover God's work around the globe even as we learn to love the people around the corner. We'll have opportunity to heal our places of pain. We'll discover new ways to love our families. We'll hear God's voice speaking into our lives as we discover new places of Influence.

IVP Crescendo invites you to join in the rising chorus

- *to listen to the voices of others*
- *to hear the voice of God*
- *and to grow your own voice in*

COURAGE. CONFIDENCE. CALLING.

ivpress.com/crescendo
ivpress.com/crescendo-social